DER *ZYKLUS HAAR*

Der HAAR-Zyklus von Angie Hiesl und Roland Kaiser besteht aus mehreren Projekten und begann 2006. Das erste Projekt, *... und HAAR und HAAR und HAAR und ...*, kam als Zusammenarbeit zwischen Angie Hiesl Produktion und dem Schauspiel Köln unter der Intendanz von Marc Günther zustande. Premiere war am 2. Juni 2006 auf dem ehemaligen Werksgelände von Klöckner Humboldt Deutz (KHD) im rechtsrheinischen Kölner Stadtteil Kalk. Der erste Teil dieses Projekts fand in einer leerstehenden, heruntergekommenen Villa, der ehemaligen Krankenstation des Werks statt – das Gebäude war aufgrund einer geplanten Straßenverlängerung bereits zum Abriss freigegeben und steht inzwischen nicht mehr. Bespielt wurden das gesamte Erdgeschoss der Villa sowie der verwilderte Garten. Nach einiger Zeit wurden die Zuschauer aus dem Garten heraus an der Außenseite der alten Fabrikationshalle entlang zu deren Hintereingang geführt. Die Halle, die heute dem Museum Ludwig als Lagerstätte dient, im wesentlichen aber leersteht, diente als Spielort für den zweiten Teil von *... und HAAR und HAAR und HAAR und ...*. Insgesamt fünfzehn Akteure sowie eine Herde Schafe nutzten die gesamte Fläche der Halle für ihre Aktionen.

Bereits auf der Düsseldorfer Tanzmesse 2004 hatten Hiesl und Kaiser über die niederländische Agentur Borneoco Kontakt zur Pekinger Künstlergruppe Living Dance Studio aufgebaut. Daraus resultierte eine Einladung, 2005 in Peking einen Workshop abzuhalten. Aus diesem Workshop ergab sich das Angebot, 2006 beim Fringe Festival in Shanghai ein Workshop-Projekt zu realisieren. Da die Recherchen für das erste Kölner HAAR-Projekt eine solche Fülle von Material erbracht hatten, dass bereits während der Arbeit der Wunsch entstanden war, das Thema HAAR weiterzuverfolgen, setzten Hiesl und Kaiser dieses Vorhaben im September 2006 bei ihrem Besuch in Shanghai in die Tat um. Nach kaum zweiwöchiger Probenzeit zeigten sie dort im Rahmen des Fringe Festivals das Projekt *...public hair...*, das als Resultat eines Workshops mit chinesischen Performern entstand und den Untertitel *work in progress* trug. Aktionsort war ein noch unbewohntes Neubauviertel in Shanghai mit Häusern für die gehobene Mittelschicht, das kurz vor der Fertigstellung stand. Während der Proben und während der Aufführung waren die Performer daher immer wieder von chinesischen Bauarbeitern umgeben.

Der Erfolg des Projekts, das während der mehrmaligen China-Aufenthalte gesammelte Material und vor allem die Nähe und das aufgebaute Vertrauen zum Living Dance Studio führten Hiesl und Kaiser zum Plan für ein größeres zweiteiliges Projekt, das die Kontinente verbinden sollte. So kam es zu *china-hair-connection Peking-Köln*, einem interdisziplinären Performanceprojekt. Wiederum begannen Hiesl und Kaiser mit einer

THE *HAIR CYCLE*

Angie Hiesl and Roland Kaiser's HAIR cycle, which consists of several projects, was launched in 2006. The first project, *... and HAIR and HAIR and HAIR and ...*, was a joint venture between Angie Hiesl Produktion and Schauspiel Köln, Cologne's municipal theater, under the directorship of Marc Günther. The première was held on 2 June 2006 in the former grounds of the engine manufacturing company Klöckner Humboldt Deutz (KHD) in Kalk, a district of Cologne on the right bank of the Rhine.

The first part of the project was staged in an empty, dilapidated villa, which was previously the works' infirmary. At the time, the building had been given a demolition order to make way for a planned road extension and is now no longer standing. The performance took place on the entire ground floor of the villa and in the overgrown garden. After a while, the audience was led out of the villa, then escorted along the outside wall of the old factory and through the back entrance into the interior of the production hall. The hall, which is now used by Museum Ludwig as a repository, served as the location for the second part of *... and HAIR and HAIR and HAIR and ...* . In all, 15 actors and a herd of sheep used the entire space available in the hall for their performances.

With the help of the Dutch agency Borneoco, Hiesl and Kaiser had already established contact with the Beijing-based artists group Living Dance Studio at the International Dance Fair in Dusseldorf in 2004. Following that meeting, Hiesl and Kaiser were invited to hold a workshop in Beijing and then subsequently asked to run a workshop project at the Fringe Festival in Shanghai in 2006. While doing research for their first HAIR project in Cologne, they had generated such a large amount of material that they decided to pursue the HAIR topic and indeed succeeded in putting their plan into action during their visit to Shanghai in September 2006. After less than two weeks of rehearsals, Hiesl and Kaiser showed the *...public hair...* project in the city as part of the Fringe Festival. This project was the outcome of a workshop with Chinese performers and was subtitled *work in progress*.

The performance was held in Shanghai in a new, upper-middle-class residential district that was almost completed but still uninhabited. During the rehearsals and the actual performance, the performers were therefore always surrounded by Chinese construction workers.

The subsequent success of the project, the vast amount of material that had been gathered during several visits to China, and, above all, the close, trusting relationship they had formed with the Living Dance Studio led Hiesl and Kaiser to plan a larger, two-part project to connect the two continents. The upshot was the interdisciplinary project *china-hair-connection Beijing-Cologne*. Here too, Hiesl and Kaiser started out by

making several research trips in preparation for the project. The outcome of their final trip, in spring 2008, was an independent conceptual photographic work entitled *Standpoint Beijing* revolving around a Chinese hairdresser's dummy with black hair. Equipped with a camera and this dummy, Hiesl and Kaiser forayed into everyday life in China. This was the start of a unique research trip that resulted in hundreds of photos, in which the hairdresser's dummy – like some foreign body – provided the only constant among a wide range of everyday scenes. For instance, the head was photographed in a sandpit, in front of two old ladies sitting resting with a dog and on a bike that was being used to transport rubbish. This sort of quirky yet at the same time minimalist – one could almost say unobtrusive – encroachment upon everyday life helped Hiesl and Kaiser to make contacts and also sensitized them to how Chinese society works and to the problems of finding artistic direction and an inner compass in a foreign country.

The location for the first part of *china-hair-connection Beijing-Cologne* in August 2008 was the Eigelstein district behind Cologne's main railway station – a typical inner-city area close to a station. During the project, the surrounding streets, squares, corners, shops and hotels were frequented by a group of European and Chinese performers.

The second part of *china-hair-connection Beijing-Cologne* took part in October 2008 in Caochangdi in northern Beijing. The district still had a distinctly villagey feel about it although it was already undergoing rapid changes. Most of the action took place in one part of the village that was made up almost entirely of brand new houses. This complex was designed by Ai Weiwei, a well-known Chinese artist whose architectural style is characterized by clear, geometric lines, purist austerity and formal stringency – in complete contrast to the chaotic, organic structure and layout of the village. The newly built-up section houses a number of contemporary art galleries, which draw the majority of visitors to the area. It is shielded by a wall from the rest of the quarter and due to the demographic background of the visitors, it is for the most part also cut off socially from the surrounding, villagey part of Caochangdi. The Chinese and Eurpean performers with whom Hiesl and Kaiser worked were the same group that had acted in Cologne. The audience was partially recruited from Beijing's art scene and many inhabitants of the village ventured out into the new gallery area, which they would otherwise never have visited, although they are not formally prohibited from doing so.

This project does not in any way mark the end of the HAIR cycle for Hiesl and Kaiser. A great deal of material still needs to be evaluated, and many images have not yet been transferred from the imaginations of their two creators into reality. Much remains to be researched – and further projects are already in the pipeline ...

Lothar Kittstein
Translated by Vivien Smith

HAAR-RISSE IN DER WIRKLICHKEIT
Zu drei Projekten von Angie Hiesl und Roland Kaiser

Unser Verhältnis zum Haar ist zutiefst ambivalent: Teil des menschlichen Körpers, in ihm verwurzelt, sind Haare dazu bestimmt, aus ihm herauszuwachsen, schließlich abzusterben und auszufallen. Volles Haar gilt als Zeichen von Potenz und Gesundheit. Verurteilte oder besiegte Feinde kahlzuscheren, ist ein uraltes Instrument der Bestrafung und Machtbekundung. Haare können auch lästig werden. Sie müssen regelmäßig geschnitten und meist täglich in Form gebracht werden, sonst wirken sie ungepflegt. Nicht zuletzt: Auf dem Großteil unseres Körpers fehlt Haar. Vom Fellkleid der Säugetiere ist beim Menschen ein mehr oder weniger sichtbarer Flaum geblieben, der kaum noch wärmt. Täglich ersetzen wir diese natürliche Barriere, die die Evolution uns genommen hat, durch Kleidung. Pelzmäntel zu tragen, ist auch ein symbolischer Sieg über das Tier, ein grausiger Versuch, die wesensmäßige Nacktheit des Homo sapiens zu verleugnen und zu verdrängen. Zugleich jedoch begehrt der Mensch Nacktheit, sie erregt ihn. Ein Tier dagegen kann gar nicht nackt sein, oder genauer: Es nimmt Nacktheit nicht wahr. Es kennt keine Lüsternheit und keine Scham.
In den drei HAAR-Projekten, die Angie Hiesl und Roland Kaiser realisiert haben, geht es immer wieder um Phänomene der Entblößung. Es geht um die Grenzen des menschlichen Körpers, und das heißt zugleich: um Grenzen, die zwischen Körpern verlaufen, um Zugriffsmöglichkeiten auf Körper, um Lust auf Körper, um Gesundheit und Krankheit von Körpern – und darum, wie all dies menschliches Leben und menschliche Lebens-Räume prägt. Ein Beispiel ist das Bild, das sich dem Zuschauer zum Auftakt des zweiten Teils von *... und HAAR und HAAR und HAAR und ...* (Köln-Kalk, 2006) bot: Fünf pelzbekleidete Akteure inmitten einer riesigen, leeren Industriehalle. Sie stehen bewegungslos, fixieren die am Rand der Halle zusammengedrängten Zuschauer mit ihren Blicken. Dann lassen sie die Mäntel fallen – und tragen nur noch ihre eigene, nackte Haut. Die entblößten Körper, begehrenswert und schutzlos zugleich, der Kälte des weitläufigen, kargen Stahl- und Ziegelbaus ausgesetzt, sind doch durch das schiere Ausmaß des leeren Raums, der sie umgibt, seltsam entrückt, vor dem schauenden Zugriff geschützt. Das Bild wirkt geradezu wie eine optische Variation auf den physikalischen Lehrsatz, wonach Luft isoliert. Tatsächlich wärmt ja ein Pelz – wie auch das Haar auf dem menschlichen Kopf – am meisten durch die Luftschicht, die zwischen Haaren Platz hat.
Und wirklich haben sich Hiesl und Kaiser in den (bisherigen) drei Projekten zum Thema Haar dreimal auf Forschungsreise in die unentdeckten Zwischen-Räume unserer Alltags- und Körperwahrnehmung begeben.

HAIR CRACKS IN REALITY
Three projects by Angie Hiesl and Roland Kaiser

Our relationship to hair is deeply ambivalent. Hair is part of the human body; rooted in the skin, it is destined to grow out from it and, ultimately, to die and fall out. A full head of hair is regarded as a sign of sexual prowess and health. Shaving the heads of convicts or defeated enemies is an ancient form of punishment and a demonstration of power. Hair can also be a nuisance. It has to be cut regularly and usually needs to be brushed into shape every day, as otherwise it looks unkempt. And not least: most of our body is not covered with hair. In humans, the only vestigial remnant of the fur that grows on mammals is a more or less visible down that provides hardly any warmth. Every day we compensate for the lack of this natural barrier, which evolution has taken away from us, by putting on clothes. Wearing a fur coat is also a symbolic victory over animals, a cruel attempt to deny and suppress the intrinsic nakedness of homo sapiens. At the same time, however, human beings desire nakedness; it excites them. An animal, on the other hand, cannot be naked or, to be more precise, it cannot perceive nakedness. It is not capable of feeling lust or shame.
The three HAIR projects realised by Angie Hiesl and Roland Kaiser deal time and again with the phenomenon of exposure. They are concerned with the boundaries of the human body, which means boundaries that run between bodies, with the possibilities of accessing bodies, with lust for bodies, with healthy bodies and with diseased bodies – and with the way all of this shapes human life and the spaces in which people live. One example is the image presented to viewers at the start of the second part of *... and HAIR and HAIR and HAIR and ...* (Cologne-Kalk, 2006). Five performers dressed in furs stand motionless in the middle of a huge, empty industrial hall, gazing at the onlookers grouped together at the edge of the hall. Then they drop their coats – and are left standing in their own, bare skin. Yet their naked bodies, which are both desirable and vulnerable, exposed as they are to the chill of the vast, bare, steel-and-brick building, are strangely disconnected and protected from the piercing gaze of the audience, due to the sheer scale of the empty space that surrounds them. This image seems almost like a visual variation on the law of physics that air has an insulating effect. Fur – like hair on the human body – keeps us warm mainly because of the layer of air that is trapped between the hairs. Indeed, in their previous three projects on hair, Hiesl and Kaiser ventured on a journey of discovery into the unexplored spaces in our everyday perception and our awareness of our bodies.

1. Körper und Raum

Im weiteren Verlauf bedecken die vierzehn Akteure von *... und HAAR und HAAR und HAAR und ...* in einer langen, stummen Aktion gemeinsam fast den gesamten Hallenboden mit menschlichen Haarresten. Sie kreieren sechszehn *Haarfelder*, parzellieren den nackten Beton und stecken dabei zugleich das Territorium für ihre Aktionen ab, die in den Feldern stattfinden werden. Dazwischen verlaufen schmale Wege für die Zuschauer. Hier liegt ein thematisches Leitmotiv der Arbeit von Hiesl und Kaiser: Sie interessieren sich für die Natur von Räumen, definieren sie um, ziehen Grenzen neu und verändern so den Blick auf unsere Lebenswelt. Zugleich aber sind die Haarfelder ein augenzwinkernder Kommentar zur Theaterkonvention – jedoch ein ambivalenter: Die Bühne als Ort künstlerischer Aktion wird durch den Aufbau der vielen, kleinen Aktionsfelder dekonstruiert, aber zugleich wieder re-affirmiert. Hiesl und Kaiser geht es nicht darum, den künstlerischen Eingriff unsichtbar zu machen, das Artifizielle der Aktion zu verleugnen. Die Projekte suchen zwar einerseits immer die *echte* Welt außerhalb der Bühne, sie suchen jedoch zugleich die Bühne in der Welt – *Bühne* verstanden als jeglicher Ort, von dem aus die gewöhnliche Realitätswahrnehmung künstlerisch in Frage gestellt werden kann.

Fünf Meter über allem hängen, an Drahtseilen hochgezogen, die Pelzmäntel: Sie begleiten den Abend wie stumme Zeugen der Gewalttat am Tier, wie ein Verweis auf den Galgen als Hinrichtungsinstrument – man kann in dem Bild aber auch den spärlichen Inhalt eines riesigen Kleiderschranks aus Stahl und Beton entdecken, den letzten Notvorrat an Kleidung für schlechte, kältere Zeiten. Das Gegenstück zu diesen leeren Kleidungshüllen, die eigentlich Häute sind, herauspräparierte Körpergrenzen ohne das, was von Natur aus ins Innere dieser Grenze gehört, ist ein Bild, das zweimal auftaucht – einmal beim ersten Kölner Projekt, einmal beim Folgeprojekt *...public hair... work in progress* in Shanghai: der (scheinbar) hüllenlose, nackte Körper einer Akteurin, der bis zu den Schultern in die Erde eingegraben ist. Die Haare sind an einem Kreis von Stöckchen festgebunden, die um den Kopf herum im Boden stecken. Auf den ersten Blick scheint die Frau mit der Umgebung zu verschmelzen, dem Erdreich verhaftet, versunken und ihrer selbst unbewusst wie eine Pflanze. Das Bild bietet scheinbar eine Momentaufnahme der ersehnten Einheit zwischen Mensch und Natur. Erst auf den zweiten Blick offenbart sich die extreme Künstlichkeit des Arrangements – und schließlich auch das Klaustrophobische der Lage der Eingegrabenen. Je näher der Zuschauer sich heranwagt, desto fester wird durch sein Gewicht das Erdreich, das den Körper der Akteurin festhält. Und doch hat das sanfte Lächeln, mit dem sie ins Leere schaut und uns einlädt, sie zu betrachten, etwas verführerisch Friedvolles, das fragt, ob nicht in der Hingabe an die Beschränkung das Glück und die Schönheit zu finden sind.

1. Body and space

In a long silent sequence in the next stage of *... and HAIR and HAIR and HAIR and ...* the fourteen performers cover almost the entire floor of the hall with hair clippings. They create sixteen *hair fields*, parcel out the bare floor and at the same time mark out the territory for their actions, which take place in the individual fields. Running between them are narrow paths for the onlookers. This is a thematic leitmotif in the work of Hiesl and Kaiser. They are interested in the nature of spaces; they redefine them, draw new boundaries and thus change our view of the world we live in. At the same time, however, the hair fields are a tongue-in-cheek commentary on theatrical convention – albeit an ambivalent one. The creation of numerous small fields of activity deconstructs the stage as a context for artistic action, but at the same time reaffirms it. Hiesl and Kaiser do not set out to make the artistic intervention invisible or to deny the artificial nature of the action. The projects always seek the *real* world beyond the stage while also seeking the stage in the world – *stage* being understood as the place from which our normal perception of reality can be questioned in an artistic way.

Five metres above all this, fur coats are suspended on wires. They accompany the evening like silent witnesses to the act of cruelty performed on animals, like a reminder of the gallows as an instrument of execution – but in this image one can also detect the meagre contents of a huge wardrobe made of steel and concrete, the last emergency store of clothing for hard, colder times. The counterpart to these empty encasings, which are actually pelts, carefully processed bodily boundaries stripped of that which naturally belongs inside, is an image that appears twice – initially in the first Cologne project and then again in the follow-up project *...public hair...* work in progress in Shanghai: the (seemingly) naked body of an actress, who is buried up to her shoulders in earth. Her hair is bound tightly to a circle of little sticks that protrude from the ground around her head. At first sight, the woman appears to blend into her environment, as if imprisoned by the earth, like a plant, subconsciously sunk into the ground and into herself. The image seems like a snapshot of the longed-for unity between mankind and nature. Only on second glance does the extreme artificiality of the arrangement emerge – and with it, ultimately, the claustrophobic nature of the situation of this woman who has been buried in the ground up to her shoulders. The closer one ventures, the firmer the soil that is trapping the performer's body becomes under the weight of one's footsteps. And yet the gentle smile with which she gazes into the middle distance and invites us to look at her has a seductive and peaceful quality, as if questioning whether happiness and beauty cannot be found in the acceptance of constraints.

In each context, however, the same image gains a different meaning. In the first part of *... and HAIR and HAIR and HAIR and ...*, in the overgrown garden of a deserted villa – a former

Dasselbe Bild gewinnt in beiden Kontexten wiederum unterschiedliche Bedeutung: Im ersten Teil von ... *und HAAR und HAAR und HAAR und ...*, im verwilderten Garten der verlassenen Kölner Villa, einer alten Krankenstation, stößt der Betrachter auf ein Arrangement wie aus dem Märchenreich, das auf seltsame Art an diesen Ort zu gehören scheint.
Bei *...public hair...* work in progress dagegen, im Garten der noch im Bau befindlichen Shanghaier Luxussiedlung für die gehobene Mittelklasse des neuen, kapitalistischen China, wirkt der Kopf, der aus der Erde ragt, wie ein Relikt, das bei den Bauarbeiten entdeckt und nicht weiter angerührt wurde, oder ein seltsames, magisches Gewächs, das sich materialisiert, sobald die Arbeiter eine Stelle erfolgreich eingeebnet und sich abgewendet haben. Ein sanfter Hinweis auf die Unverdrängbarkeit der anarchischen Kräfte der Natur. Ein irritierender Gegenpol zur lauten Geschäftigkeit der Umgebung und zur Glätte der frisch verputzten Mauern. Zugleich aber, gerade für chinesische Zuschauer, ein politischer Verweis auf das Thema Gewalt, Einkerkerung und Folter – auf die Schattenseiten des chinesischen Wirtschaftswunders.
Immer wieder stoßen Hiesl und Kaiser, wenn sie das menschliche Verhältnis zum Haar untersuchen, auf das Verhältnis zur Um- und Mitwelt – zu den Räumen, in denen Menschen sich einrichten (müssen), und zu den Grenzen, die diese Räume prägen. So im ersten, im Kölner Teil von *china-hair-connection Peking-Köln*: Hier agiert eine chinesische Tänzerin vor dem Fenster einer Bäckerei in der nicht gerade ansehnlichen Gegend hinter dem Kölner Hauptbahnhof. Sie taucht ihr langes Haar in rote Wassereimer, klatscht das nasse Haar mit Wucht gegen die Scheibe und wischt dann das Glas mit ihrem Haar wie mit einem schwarzen Lappen sauber, immer und immer wieder. In diesem Bild mischen sich Schönheit und Kraft der ritualisierten Bewegung mit dem Eindruck von Vergeblichkeit, ja Zwang. Der Vorgang wirkt, je länger man zusieht, immer stärker wie ein vergebliches Anrennen, ja wie der zum Scheitern verurteilte Versuch, eine Grenze zu durchbrechen, zwischen den Materialien Haar, Wasser und Glas eine Verbindung herzustellen. Dasselbe Thema variiert ein anderes Bild aus *china-hair-connection Peking-Köln*: Im Geäst einer alten Platane agieren eine europäische Performerin und ein chinesischer Performer mit Teig, sie kneten ihn durch, lassen ihn in langen Bahnen über die Äste, die eigenen Körper laufen, ziehen ihn wieder hoch, ballen ihn zusammen, kneten ihn durch und lassen ihn wieder herunterlaufen. Teig und Wasser sind Lebensmittel, doch beide wirken selbst seltsam kalt und unbelebt, sind Stoffe, die eben nie wirklich in den Menschen eindringen, sondern – in der Performance – nur auf ihm liegen oder – beim Verzehr – durch ihn hindurchgehen. Die Schichten des Teigs schmiegen sich der lebendigen Haut bzw. Baumrinde nur an, sie scheinen sie zu umschmeicheln, aber verschmelzen nicht mit ihr.
Wer sich am Ort der Kölner Aktion umsieht, dem fällt auf, dass der massive Baum am Rande einer Brücke wächst, unter

infirmary – in Cologne, the spectator stumbles upon a fairy-tale-like arrangement that seems to belong to this place in a strange way. In *...public hair...* work in progress, on the other hand, in the grounds of the luxury Shanghai development for the upper middle class of the new capitalist China, the head protruding from the earth seems like a relic that was discovered during construction work and never touched again – or like some strange, magical plant that materialises as soon as the workers have successfully levelled off one area and turned their backs on it. A subtle reference to the irrepressibility of the anarchic forces of nature – a disconcerting antithesis to the noisy activity of the surroundings and the freshly plastered walls. At the same time, however, particularly for Chinese viewers, it is a political allusion to the issue of violence, imprisonment and torture – and to the dark side of China's economic miracle.
When examining the human response to hair, Hiesl and Kaiser repeatedly confront people's relationship with their surroundings and their environment – with the spaces in which they (have to) make themselves at home and to the boundaries that characterise these spaces. This is evident in the first part of *china-hair-connection Beijing-Cologne*. In Cologne, a Chinese dancer performs in front of the window of a bakery in the not-so-respectable district behind Cologne's main railway station. She dips her long hair into red buckets filled with water and then, with a flick of her head, forcefully slaps her wet tresses against the window pane. She then wipes the glass clean with her hair as if it were a black cloth, and repeats the action again and again. In this image, the beauty and power of the ritualised movement merge with the impression of futility, if not of compulsion. The longer one watches this event, the more the performer seems to be making a desperate attempt, which is doomed to failure, to break through a boundary between the three materials – hair, water and glass. Another image from *china-hair-connection Beijing-Cologne* is a variation on the same theme. In the branches of an old plane tree, two performers – one European and one Chinese – act out a scene with dough. They knead it, draping it in long strips over the branches and their own bodies, pull it up again, roll it into a ball, knead it and let it drop down again. Dough and water contain vital nutrients but both seem strangely cold and inanimate. During the performance, these materials never really permeate the human body but are merely draped on top of it during the performance, or pass through it if they are consumed. The layers of dough only cling to living skin or to the bark of a tree. They appear to envelop it, but they do not fuse with it.
No one looking around on the fringes of the Cologne performance can fail to notice the massive tree growing on the edge of a bridge over a multi-lane road. The ground in which the tree is rooted is hollowed out and covers a high-speed transit area, a space that is hostile to life. The obsessive slowness and tenderness with which the actors handle the dough also forms a

der eine vielspurige Autounterführung verläuft. Der Grund selbst, in dem er wurzelt, ist wenige Meter weiter ausgehöhlt und überdeckt einen Raum des Transits, der Hochgeschwindigkeit, der Lebensfeindlichkeit. Auch im Kontrast zu dieser automobilen Unterwelt ist die obsessive, zärtliche Langsamkeit zu sehen, mit der die Akteure den Teig behandeln. So wird das scheinbar einfache Bild letztlich zu einer Reflexion über Natürlichkeit und Künstlichkeit, über Langsamkeit und Geschwindigkeit, über Nähe und Distanz im städtischen Raum. Die Teigbilder, die es auf Kölner Straßen und auch in Peking – dort mit langen chinesischen Nudeln – mehrfach gab, sind eine Variation über menschliche Aneignung von Welt, über das unlösbare Verhältnis von Einverleibung und Abgrenzung.

In allen drei Projekten begegnet man Bildern mit menschlichem Haar in verschiedenen Farben, Längen und Qualitäten – ob als offenes Wirrhaar, als Strähnchen und Bündel zusammengefasst oder als Tressen zusammengenäht (die Grundlage für Haarverlängerungen, Verdichtungen und Haarersatz). Das Haar wird auf Wegen ausgelegt, auf Leinen getrocknet, an Wände geklebt. Barbiepuppen hängen an ihren *eigenen* Haaren an Wänden oder stehen zu hunderten in Regalen oder auf Wegen – anatomisch grotesk verdreht, so dass ihre Scham nach oben zeigt, die von Performerinnen mit schwarzem Echthaar beklebt worden ist. Die sonst hüftabwärts geschlechtslosen, sterilen Puppen gewinnen dadurch ein gespenstisches Leben. Haar füllt in diesen Bildern Flächen und Wände, nimmt sich Raum, raut ihn auf, verlebendigt ihn, macht ihn aber auch unpassierbar, füllt die Luft mit kleinsten Staub- und Gewebepartikeln, verströmt eine Aura von beißender Trockenheit. In einem Bild, das in beiden Teilen von *china-hair-connection Peking-Köln* auftaucht, füllen Haarreste ganze Badewannen (ein Raum für Feuchtes) und wirbeln durch die Luft, sobald die Akteure in den Wannen tanzen. Haar verändert in all diesen Bildern Räume und Flächen auf so irritierende Weise, weil hierdurch erst deutlich wird, wo in unserer alltäglichen Wahrnehmung Haar *keinen* Platz hat. Die Bilder stoßen uns darauf, wie stark die Zivilisation unsere Wahrnehmung an glatte Flächen gewöhnt hat, an Flächen ohne Ornament und ohne jede echte Unregelmäßigkeit. Haarteppiche und Haarspuren stellen – gerade im städtischen und industriellen Raum – den Primat der Geradlinigkeit in Frage. Zugleich aber, und das ist für die Arbeitsweise von Hiesl und Kaiser zentral, respektieren diese Bilder stets die Grenze zwischen dem künstlerischen Eingriff und dem Ding, das dessen Objekt ist. Das Haar, das die Mauern bedeckt, bleibt in Hiesls und Kaisers Bildern meist absichtlich schütter, es will den Gegenstand, der verändert wird, eben nicht umwandeln oder verbergen, es macht ihn in seiner Eigenart erst auf neue Art sichtbar. Selbst der in klinisches Weiß getauchte Kölner Bahnbrücken-Bogen aus *china-hair-connection Peking-Köln*, in dem eine Akteurin mit fast bodenlangem Haar sich ganz ruhig daran macht, die Zweige von Apfelbäumchen mit roten Schnüren am Boden festzubinden, thematisiert

contrast to this automobile underworld. The seemingly simple image ultimately becomes a reflection on naturalness and artificiality, on slowness and speed, on closeness and distance in an urban setting. The dough images that are created several times on Cologne streets and also in Beijing (with long Chinese noodles) are a variation on humankind's appropriation of the world, on the insoluble relationship between assimilation and delineation.

In all three projects, one encounters images with human hair of different colours, lengths and qualities – whether it is hair gathered in strands or bunches or sewn together as tresses that form the basis for hair extensions, hair thickening or artificial hair for wigs and toupees. The hair is laid out on paths, dried on linen or stuck to walls. Barbie dolls are suspended from walls by their *own* hair, while hundreds of them are arranged on shelves or on paths – their anatomies grotesquely distorted, and their pudenda, onto which the women performers have stuck real black hair, facing upwards. The sterile dolls, which are otherwise asexual from the hips down, thus assume a ghostly persona. In these images, hair covers empty spaces and walls, takes over space, roughens it up, brings it to life but also makes it impassable, fills the air with the tiniest particles of dust and tissue and exudes a dry, pungent aura. In one image, which occurs in both parts of *china-hair-connection Beijing-Cologne*, hair clippings fill entire bath tubs (usually considered a wet environment) and swirl through the air as soon as the actors dance in the tubs. In all these images, the way in which hair thus transforms spaces and areas is disconcerting because it shows clearly where hair does *not* belong in our daily perception. The images make us aware of the extent to which civilisation has accustomed our perception to smooth surfaces, to surfaces without ornamentation and without any real irregularity, while hair carpets and hair traces – especially in urban and industrial spaces – question the primacy of rectilinearity. At the same time, however, and this is central to Hiesl and Kaiser's method of working, these images always respect the boundary between the artistic intervention and its target. In Hiesl and Kaiser's images, the hair that covers the walls usually remains deliberately sparse. It does not aim to transform or conceal the object that is thus altered. Rather, in its uniqueness, it makes it visible in a new way. In one scene in *china-hair-connection Beijing-Cologne*, which takes place in an arched underpass belonging to Cologne's train system, a female performer whose hair reaches almost to the ground quite calmly sets about tying the branches of miniature apple trees to the ground with red ribbons. This tidying and taming action, set against a clinically white background, focuses our attention on the process of shaping open spaces and nature. It is no coincidence that in Hiesl and Kaiser's projects, trees are not sawed into pieces or burned. In the performance, the violence that befalls things is insolubly mixed with carefulness, indeed tenderness and devotion and respect for their uniqueness.

in dieser Ordnungs- und Zähmungsaktion den Vorgang der Gestaltung von Raum und Natur selbst. Es ist kein Zufall, dass bei Hiesl und Kaiser die Bäumchen nicht zersägt oder verbrannt werden: In der Aktion mischen sich unauflösbar Gewalt, die den Dingen widerfährt, und Sorgfalt, ja Zärtlichkeit und Hingabe, Achtung vor ihrer Eigenart.

2. China und Deutschland

Die Veränderung von Räumen und Körpern durch Haare – oder in vielen Bildern auch: durch das Scheren und Entfernen von Haar – versucht eben nicht, die *wahre Natur* von Räumen und Gegenständen aufzudecken, sie schärft vielmehr möglichst den Blick für all das, was in und hinter den Dingen liegt. Der künstlerische Eingriff macht auf Grenzziehungen aufmerksam, die menschliches Leben und menschliche Orte prägen, auf die Tatsache, dass es keinen Ort gibt, an dem Menschen leben, der nicht ständig verwandelt wird, aber eben auch keinen Ort, den Menschen je wirklich kontrollieren könnten. In diesem Sinne heißt *site-specific work* für Hiesl und Kaiser weder, sich dem Charakter eines Orts anzupassen, noch einen behaupteten *eigentlichen* Charakter herauszuarbeiten – es bedeutet vielmehr, mit den verborgenen *Möglichkeiten* von Orten zu spielen. Ein Beispiel ist der zweite, Pekinger Teil von *china-hair-connection Peking-Köln*: Das Projekt fand in einem Außenbezirk statt, der noch stark dörflichen Charakter hat. Am Rand dieses Dorfs entsteht, umgeben von einer Mauer, ein Neubauviertel aus architektonisch gleichförmigen Neubauten, in denen vor allem Kunstgalerien untergebracht sind; ein räumlich, baulich, kulturell und sozial dem umgebenden Dorf radikal entgegengesetzter Raum. Zum Auftakt des Projekts stellen Hiesl und Kaiser nicht etwa die Trennung beider Bereiche demonstrativ in Frage. Vielmehr hocken auf der Mauer in größeren Abständen ganz einfach Akteure und schauen ruhig, teils rauchend hinaus. Die grundlegende künstlerische Geste der *site-specific work* ist der offene Blick, Wahrnehmung, die weder einlädt noch ausschließt, die materielle und soziale Grenzen nicht bewertet, sondern zuallererst bemerkbar macht. Nicht zufällig bestand das einzige Bild des Projekts, das im dörflichen Teil des Viertels angesiedelt war, aus einer einzelnen Performerin, die, schick angezogen, am Straßenrand neben einem tragbaren Radiogerät hockte – und schaute.

Der deutsche Blick auf China ist traditionell widersprüchlich. China gilt als rätselhaft, exotisch, sinnlich, verlockend – Chinesen dagegen gelten als diszipliniert, duldsam und überhöflich. Zugleich ist chinesisches Haar mit seiner satten schwarzen Farbe ein Inbegriff von Kraft, Fülle und Gesundheit. Tatsächlich ist Echthaar aus China für den europäischen Markt meist ungeeignet – weil die Haare zu dick sind! Zugleich begegnet dem künstlerischen Blick in China selbst eine brüchige, vielgestaltige Realität, deren Prinzip geradezu die Gleichzeitigkeit des Gegensätzlichen zu sein scheint: Armut und Reichtum, glitzernde Wolkenkratzer und ärmliche Dörfer, stürmische Ver-

2. China and Germany

Changing spaces and bodies through the use of hair – or in many of Hiesl and Kaiser's images, also by cutting and removing hair – is not an attempt to reveal the *true nature* of spaces and objects. Rather, this aims to heighten our awareness of what lies in and behind things. The artistic intervention makes one aware of the drawing of boundaries that shape human life and the places where we live – and of the fact that there is no place where people live that is not being constantly changed. Nor is there any place that people could ever really keep in check. In this sense, for Hiesl and Kaiser, *site-specific work* means neither adapting to the character of a place nor working out its alleged *true* character. On the contrary, it means playing with the hidden *possibilities* that places offer. One example of this occurs in the second part of *china-hair-connection Beijing-Cologne* in the Chinese capital. The project took place in an outlying district of the city that still has a distinctly villagey feel. On the edge of the village, surrounded by a wall, a new quarter with architecturally uniform buildings, most of which house art galleries, is taking shape – an area that forms a dramatic contrast to the surrounding village – in spatial, architectural, social and cultural terms.

At the beginning of the project, Hiesl and Kaiser deliberately do not question the separation of these two areas. Rather, performers simply squat on the wall at large intervals and gaze steadily ahead, sometimes smoking. The underlying artistic gesture of *site-specific work* is an open look, a perception which neither invites nor excludes, which does not evaluate material or social boundaries but first and foremost brings them to our attention. It is no coincidence that the only image in the project based in a villagey part of the quarter consisted of one single performer, smartly dressed, squatting at the side of the road beside a portable radio – and looking around.

Germans' view of China is contradictory. Traditionally, China is regarded as enigmatic, exotic, sensual and enticing, while the Chinese are seen as disciplined, patient and over-polite. At the same time, Chinese hair with its rich dark colour epitomises strength, fitness and health. In fact, real hair from China is generally unsuitable for the European market because the hair is too thick. Meanwhile, in China itself, when one attempts to approach the subject of hair from an artistic point of view, one comes face to face with a brittle, diverse reality, which appears to be based on the simultaneity of contrasts: poverty and wealth, gleaming skyscrapers and poor villages, dramatic changes and tenacious tradition. Yet while political expression is strictly reglemented in China, if not taboo, urban public and private spaces permeate one another in a manner to which Europeans are not accustomed. One often sees dining tables and cooking stoves in front of houses on the street. The new quarter that was available for *china-hair-connection Beijing-Cologne* is also a semi-private, semi-public space, except in reverse: although the space is not expressly off-limits for the

änderung und beharrliche Tradition. Politische Äußerungen sind in China stark reglementiert, ja tabuisiert – zugleich aber durchdringen sich urbaner öffentlicher und privater Raum auf eine für Europäer ganz ungewohnte Art. So stehen oft Esstische und Öfen, auf denen gekocht wird, noch vor dem Haus an der Straße. Ein halbprivater, halböffentlicher Raum ist auch das Neubau-Viertel, das am Rande des Pekinger Vorort-Dorfs für *china-hair-connection Peking-Köln* zur Verfügung stand, nur umgekehrt: Den Dorfbewohnern ist das Areal zwar nicht ausdrücklich, aber doch faktisch – durch die unsichtbaren Schranken der kulturellen und sozialen Differenz – unzugänglich. Es ist ein öffentlicher Ort, den man nicht aufsucht.

Ein Bild, das Hiesl und Kaiser in einem Innenhof des ummauerten Bezirks kreierten, wirkt wie ein Kommentar auf die räumlichen und sozialen Verwerfungen, die das neue China durchziehen: Aus der Tür eines der schmucklosen Backsteinquader, der erst im Rohbau steht, ergießt sich eine riesige Kaskade roter Lampions bis weit in den Hof hinein. Aus der kargen, schnell hochgezogenen Kulisse des Neuen bricht, nicht zu bändigen und in all seiner rätselhaften Schönheit, als irrlichterndes Ornament das Alte hervor – und erstarrt doch auf seinem Weg notwendig, bleibt als Bild unbewegt, eingegossen in die bauliche Form des Neuen. Der Eingriff bleibt Zitat, Klischee – und macht sich doch absichtsvoll als solches kenntlich. Die Lampions, die mit den Troddeln, die sie tragen, selbst über eine Art *Haarschopf* verfügen, zitieren das alte China, verweisen in ihrer Vielzahl jedoch zugleich auf die moderne Massenproduktion, sie sind im Vergleich zu den umgebenden Gebäuden ornamental-verspielt und bei näherem Hinsehen standardisiert und normiert zugleich.

Ein ähnliches und doch ganz neues Bild schufen Hiesl und Kaiser für den ersten, den Kölner Teil von *china-hair-connection Peking-Köln*: Eine Akteurin entfaltet im Innenraum eines geparkten Autos allmählich immer mehr rote Lampions – bis das Wageninnere vollständig ausgefüllt ist. Auch hier bedient sich die Kunst der Widersprüchlichkeit des Objekts, das leuchtende Fülle, sinnliche Versuchung symbolisiert und doch in zusammengefaltetem Zustand zeigt, dass es wenig mehr ist als ein rotes Stück Stoff. Die Lampions repräsentieren Leere und Fülle zugleich, sie füllen das deutsche Auto am Straßenrand bis zum Bersten – mit einem Nichts aus Farbe und Luft. Sie zeigen, wie trügerisch Volumen und Materie überhaupt sind. Zugleich ist das Bild ein augenzwinkernder Verweis auf die Flüchtigkeit des Glücks; denn die roten Lampions sind in China auch Glückssymbol. Nicht zufällig bleibt das Auto im deutschen Kontext geschlossen, es entsteht keine Kaskade, der Metallhülle des Fahrzeugs gelingt es, das widerspenstige Material im Inneren zu umklammern. Und doch wird das Auto, das für den unachtsamen Passanten gar nicht verändert erscheint, durch die Lampions im Inneren verwandelt.

Wie Haar von innen nach außen immer neu nachwächst, bewegen sich die Haar-Projekte zwischen geschlossenen und

village residents, in effect it is because of the invisible barriers created by cultural and social differences. It is a public space that people do not seek to go to.

One image that Hiesl and Kaiser erected in an inner courtyard in the walled quarter seems like a commentary on the spatial and social distortions that pervade the new China. A huge cascade of red lanterns pours out from the door of one of the bare brick buildings which is still under construction – and spills into the courtyard. Out of the bare, quickly erected backdrop of the new, the old bursts forth like a jack o' lantern ornament that cannot be tamed in all its enigmatic beauty – and yet necessarily freezes in the process, remaining as an unmoving image, cast into the architectural form of the new. The intervention remains a mere quote – a cliché – and deliberately identifies itself as such. The lanterns, whose tassles are like shocks of hair, are a reference to the old China, but in their large numbers they also refer to modern mass production. In contrast to the surrounding buildings, they are ornamental and playful, but when one looks closer they are standardized and normed.

Hiesl and Kaiser created a similar and yet entirely new image for the first part of *china-hair-connection Beijing-Cologne*, which was performed in Cologne. A woman performer, seated in a parked car, gradually unfolds more and more red paper lanterns – until the car's interior is completely filled with them. Here, too, art exploits the contradictions of the object which, filled with light, symbolises sensual temptation and yet, in its folded state shows that it is little more than a piece of red fabric. The lanterns represent emptiness and fullness at one and the same time; they fill the German car at the side of the road until it is ready to burst. They show how totally deceptive volume and material are. At the same time, the image is a tongue-in-cheek reference to the transience of happiness, red lanterns being a symbol of luck in China. It is no coincidence that the car in the German context remains closed. There is no cascade of lanterns here. The metal shell of the car succeeds in embracing the unmanageable material inside. And yet the car, which to the unobservant passer-by does not appear changed in any way, is transformed from the inside by the lanterns.

Just as hair continues to grow from the inside to the outside, the hair projects move to and fro between enclosed and open spaces; they jump from the otherwise inaccessible factory hall to the exclusive Chinese residential area (which, however, is still a construction site and not really *public*) to the centre of the maze of streets around the Eigelstein quarter, close to Cologne's main railway station. This, too, is a place of transition, of contradictions, which one hurries through to get to the station or the city centre. It is an area with typical Cologne pubs and kebab shops, an unofficial red light district, a quarter with a long tradition, full of transient shops selling cheap goods. Hectic activity alongside empty access streets without shops, a mediaeval city gate and railway underpasses. Transi-

öffentlichen Räumen hin und her, springen von der sonst unzugänglichen Fabrikhalle zum exklusiven chinesischen Wohnviertel (das aber noch Baustelle und nicht eigentlich *öffentlich* ist), dann mitten ins Straßengewirr um den Eigelstein in Kölns Bahnhofsgegend. Auch dies ist wieder ein Ort des Übergangs und der Widersprüche, durch den man zum Bahnhof, in die Innenstadt eilt, ein Viertel der kölschen Kneipen und Kebabbuden, ein inoffizieller Rotlichtbezirk, ein Traditionsviertel voller kurzlebiger Ramschläden. Hektische Betriebsamkeit neben toten Zulieferstraßen ohne Geschäfte, eine mittelalterliche Torburg, Bahnunterführungen. Das Transitorische als Element, das letztlich jedem Raum eignet, prägt alle drei HAAR-Projekte, wie es auch das Phänomen Haar auszeichnet: Haar haben wir immer nur vorläufig, es muss ständig gepflegt werden, um schön zu sein. Und dagegen, dass es im Alter irgendwann schütter wird, ist bislang noch kein Kraut gewachsen.

Darum macht die in allen möglichen Formen immer aufs Neue ausagierte Pflege von Haar in allen Projekten einen wichtigen Teil der Bilder aus, mit denen Hiesl und Kaiser arbeiten – ob ein Tangopaar während des Tanzes sein Haar einshampooniert, ob eine Akteurin Haartressen sorgsam wäscht und danach zum Trocknen aufhängt, oder ob Akteure Haarbüschel aufwändig zu rechteckigen Haarfeldern ordnen. Letztlich sind es Reste der Haarindustrie, die hier verwendet und künstlerisch recycelt werden: Waren – zugleich aber *Menschen-Material*, Teile menschlicher Körper, und deshalb ist die künstlerische Haltung ihnen gegenüber zuallererst ein hoher Respekt. Es ist kein Zufall, dass in allen drei Projekten kein einziges Bild vorkommt, in dem Haar absichtlich verschmutzt oder entwürdigt wird. Im Garten der Krankenstation auf dem alten Kölner Industriegelände, das Spielort für ... *und HAAR und HAAR und HAAR und* ... war, gab es einen zweiten Akteur, der in die Erde eingegraben war und mit einem Feuerzeug einzelne Haarsträhnen verbrannte. Die Aktion erscheint aber nicht als Akt der Zerstörung. Vielmehr liegt in der langsamen, sorgfältigen Aktion geradezu Ehrerbietung, ja stille Andacht. Das gilt auch für andere von Hiesl und Kaiser kreierte Bilder, z.B. noch eines aus ... *und HAAR und HAAR und HAAR und* ...: Eine Akteurin, die krankheitsbedingt am ganzen Körper haarlos ist, klebt ganz allmählich und in aller Ruhe mit rotem Klebeband kleine Haarsträhnchen auf ihrem nackten Körper fest. Die Entblößung des eigenen Zustands – der in unserer Gesellschaft allgemein als unattraktiv gilt – ist potenziell erniedrigend, wird durch die Gelassenheit, mit der der Vorgang ausgeführt wird jedoch zu einer souveränen Reflexion über den Blick der Zuschauenden selbst. So diente auch die methodische Verbrennung kleinster Mengen von Menschenhaar eben nicht der Provokation. In dem Bild liegt vielmehr so etwas wie ein Echo des Opferritus, bei dem sich in weiten Teilen Südasiens Gläubige mit einer Bitte an die Götter in Tempeln kahlscheren lassen. Das Haar wird dann zum Opfer, und das heißt: zur Bezah-

toriness as an element that ultimately applies to any space also characterises all three HAIR projects, as it does the phenomenon of hair. We only ever have hair temporarily; it always has to be looked after in order to be beautiful. And as yet, nothing can be done about the fact that in old age it becomes thin. That is why hair care, in all its possible forms, is acted out again and again. In all the projects, it is an important part of the images with which Hiesl and Kaiser work – whether it is a couple dancing the tango and shampooing their hair during the dance, a female performer carefully washing tresses and then hanging them up to dry or performers elaborately organising the bunches of hair in rectangular hair *fields*. Ultimately, it is the *leftovers* of the hair industry that are being used here and recycled for art. Goods – but at the same time *human material*, a part of the human body, which is why the artistic attitude towards hair is first and foremost one of great respect. It is no coincidence that in all three projects there is not a single image in which hair is deliberately dirtied or degraded. In the garden of the infirmary in the old industrial site in Cologne, the venue for ... *and HAIR and HAIR and HAIR and* ... a second actor was buried up to his armpits in the ground, burning individual strands of hair with a cigarette lighter. However, the action does not appear destructive. Rather, in its slow, careful execution, it expresses reverence, if not silent devotion. The same also applies to other images created by Hiesl and Kaiser, for example, in ... *and HAIR and HAIR and HAIR and* ...: A female performer, who has no hair on her body due to illness, calmly and gradually sticks small strands of hair to her naked body with red sticky tape. The exposure of her own condition, which our society regards as unattractive, is potentially degrading, but thanks to the serenity with which the action is performed, it becomes a calm and collected reflection on the way in which onlookers view the world around them. Likewise, the methodical burning of the tiniest amounts of human hair does not appear provocative. Rather the image contains more of an echo of the sacrificial ritual in which believers in many parts of South Asia have their heads shaved and appeal to the gods in temples. Hair thus becomes a sacrifice, payment for a reward from the gods. In fact, the hair thus acquired returns to the global economic cycle and trade with hair. It ends up as hair pieces and wigs in the rich countries of the west, thereby generating both worldly and spiritual capital.

3. Standstill and movement
The burning of strands of hair – seen in the context of the earth that has been excavated and the actor who has been dug into the ground – awakens associations with sacrifice, prayer and burial and points to two central issues dealt with in the hair projects: transience and concentration. Both these terms aptly describe Hiesl and Kaiser's method of working. In the projects, their art does not lay claim to any lasting value. It

lung für göttliche Gegenleistung. Tatsächlich wandert das so gewonnene Haar wiederum in den weltweiten wirtschaftlichen Kreislauf des Haars, es landet in Form von Haarteilen und Perücken in den reichen Ländern des Westens, es generiert ebenso weltliches wie spirituelles Kapital.

3. Stillstand und Bewegung

Indem die Verbrennung von Haarsträhnen – im Zusammenspiel mit dem ausgehobenen Erdreich und dem eingegrabenen Akteur – die Assoziationsfelder Opfer, Andacht und Begräbnis öffnet, verweist sie auf zwei Kernthemen der HAAR-Projekte: Vergänglichkeit und Konzentration. Die beiden Begriffe beschreiben Hiesls und Kaisers Arbeitsweise recht gut: Ihre Kunst beansprucht in den Projekten keinen Ewigkeitswert, sie verwandelt Räume vorübergehend und zieht sich aus ihnen auch wieder zurück. Sie gewinnt ihre Kraft aus dem Transitorischen. Für kurze Zeit konzentrieren sich in den Bildern des jeweiligen Projekts diskursive Kraftfelder und untergründige räumliche Konflikte, arrangieren sich neu und überdauern schließlich nur im Bewusstsein der Zuschauer und Passanten, die jeweils unterschiedliche Ausschnitte und Bild-Folgen wahr- und mit nach Hause nehmen.

Menschliches Haar fällt täglich anders. Temperatur, Luftfeuchtigkeit, Stimmungen, Tagesform – jeder Mensch, der noch Haare besitzt, hat eine Frisur, aber sie sieht jeden Morgen anders aus. Ein *bad hair day*, so heißt im Englischen ein Tag, an dem die Haare schlecht liegen, kann psychisch zur echten Belastung werden. Haar ist unberechenbar, es muss zurechtgemacht werden. Natürlichkeit und Künstlichkeit sind beim Haar keine einfachen Gegensätze, sondern untrennbar verbunden. So elementar die Attraktion durch Haar auch ist, so stolz wir auf unser Haar sein mögen – es bleibt ein Geschenk der Natur, und das heißt paradoxerweise: es bedeutet Arbeit. Der Mensch, der sich morgens zurechtmacht, seine Haare mit Kamm, Bürste, Gel, Spray in Form bringt, durchläuft zugleich den Prozess der Zivilisation, von der ungeformten Wildheit des *out of bed*-Look (heute auch mit besonderem Gel künstlich herzustellen) hin zur gebändigten Schönheit des Gesellschaftswesens. Die Haarwesen, die sich durch Hiesls und Kaisers Projekte bewegen, mal kahlgeschoren, mal nackt und am Körper mit Haarsträhnchen beklebt, mal unter einem Berg von Haar regelrecht begraben, brechen diesen Prozess auf, vollziehen ihn nach, machen ihn rückgängig, spiegeln ihn, zerlegen ihn in seine Bestandteile. Die Akteure verschönern sich und entstellen sich, sie dekorieren den Raum, in dem sie agieren, und lassen ihn uns zugleich un-heimlich werden, sie legen seine Fallstricke offen und dringen in seine verborgenen Schönheiten vor, sie zeigen die unaufhebbare Verbindung von Form und Zerfall, und letztlich: die nicht hintergehbare Vorläufigkeit menschlichen Lebens und Handelns.

Das Transitorische als Grundzug der *conditio humana* – das ist vielleicht eine Quintessenz des Themas Haar, wie es in den

simply transforms spaces temporarily and then withdraws from them again. It gains its power from the transitory. For a short time, discursive energy fields and underlying spatial conflicts are concentrated in the images, which then rearrange themselves and ultimately remain merely in the minds of the onlookers and passers-by who, for their part, ultimately perceive and take home with them different excerpts and series of images.

Human hair falls differently every day. It is affected by temperature, air humidity, moods and one's individual form. Anyone who still has hair has a hairstyle, but it looks different every day. A *bad hair day* can produce real mental anguish. Hair is unpredictable, it has to be *done*. When it comes to hair, naturalness and artificiality are not mere contrasts but are inextricably linked. As basic as the attraction of hair may be and however proud we may be of our hair, it remains a gift of nature and, paradoxically, that means that it involves work. A person who gets ready in the morning, who *does* his or her hair with a comb, a brush, gel or spray, goes through the process of civilisation, from the unkempt wildness of the just-out-of-bed look (which nowadays can be achieved artificially with the aid of a special gel) through to the tamed beauty befitting a social being. The *hair beings* that move through Hiesl and Kaiser's projects, sometimes with their heads shaved, sometimes naked and with strands of hair stuck to their bodies, sometimes literally buried under a mountain of hair, prise open this process, comprehend it, reverse it, reflect it, break it down into its individual components. The performers make themselves more attractive, and deface themselves; they decorate the space in which they are acting, and at the same time make it uncomfortable for us. They reveal its pitfalls and penetrate its hidden beauties. They show the irreversible connection between form and disintegration and, ultimately, the undeniable transience of human life and activity.

Transitoriness as a basic feature of the human condition is perhaps the quintessence of the theme of hair as it appears in the three projects that Hiesl and Kaiser have realized to date. This is evident in the seemingly static image of the female performer who has been *dug into* the ground. Surrounded by a halo of her hair, she commands an almost regal, Madonna-like authority – at the expense of having her body imprisoned. The baffling image of the sunken beauty can only be achieved by means that harm the human body. The unfamiliarity of the image is an open reference to the process of its creation and also to the work that will be needed to free the performer at the end of the day. The effort that was exerted in order to create a state of total deadlock retains in the image a sort of kinetic energy that accounts for its fascinating and disturbing beauty. In that sense, it is also no coincidence that *Hair* is not the name of one single project but of a series of projects that shifts geographically between continents. It is not surprising that, while researching the topic of hair, Hiesl and Kaiser were

drei Projekten erscheint, die Hiesl und Kaiser bisher dazu realisiert haben. Das zeigt sich selbst in dem scheinbar statischen Bild der im Boden *vergrabenen* Performerin: Umgeben vom Strahlenkranz ihres Haars, behauptet sie eine königinnengleiche, madonnenhafte Herrschaft über die Umgebung – um den Preis der Gefangenschaft ihres Körpers. Das rätselhafte Bild der versunkenen Schönheit lässt sich nur erzeugen durch Maßnahmen, die dem menschlichen Körper Gewalt antun, die Fremdheit des Bildes verweist offen auf den Prozess seiner Erzeugung und auch auf die Arbeit, die nötig sein wird, um die Akteurin am Ende des Tages wieder zu befreien. Die Mühe, die aufgewendet wurde, um einen Zustand absoluten Stillstands zu erzeugen, hinterlässt in dem Bild eine Art kinetischer Energie und erzeugt so erst seine faszinierende und verstörende Schönheit.

In diesem Sinne ist es auch kein Zufall, dass *Haar* nicht der Titel eines einzelnen Projekts, sondern einer Reihe ist, die sich geographisch zwischen den Kontinenten bewegt. Nicht umsonst entdeckten Hiesl und Kaiser bei ihren Recherchen zum Thema *Haar* mit Begeisterung und Faszination die Verbindungen nach Asien und insbesondere zur chinesischen Kultur. Wie von selbst sucht sich *Haar* Räume des Übergangs, des Nichtmehr oder des Noch-nicht-ganz. Der Weg beginnt in einer leeren Hülle des untergegangenen europäischen Industriezeitalters, folgt dem Pfad der westlichen Sehnsucht nach dem Orient mit seinem schwarzen, dicken Haar, geheimnisvollen Tempeln, unbekannten Düften, gerät in das soziale Gemisch der Kölner Bahnhofsgegend, in der sich im Dienstleistungszeitalter deutsche Kneipenkultur mit dem Geruch von Kebab und dem Neonlicht der Billigläden verbindet, die fernöstliches Plastikspielzeug anbieten, und endet schließlich im wilden Gestrüpp des ungestümen kommunistisch-kapitalistischen Wachstums der chinesischen Städte, die die dörfliche Welt an ihren Außenrändern allmählich einsaugen und verschlucken. Haar ist für Hiesl und Kaiser kein begrenztes *Thema*, zu dem eine künstlerische These zu formulieren wäre. Vielmehr wird *Haar* in ihrer Arbeit zum Schlüssel für die künstlerische Erkundung des Welt-Raums, in dem wir leben. So wie uns täglich Haare ausfallen, die sich in den Ritzen zwischen unseren Möbeln, im Flor unserer Teppiche und in den Abflüssen unserer Duschkabinen festsetzen, so setzen sich Partikel des Themas *Haar* durch Hiesls und Kaisers Arbeitsweise in den unvorhersehbarsten und verstecktesten Winkeln unseres Alltags und unseres kulturellen Bewusstseins ab. Das macht die Auseinandersetzung mit dem Phänomen Haar für den Betrachter zu einer Konfrontation mit gesellschaftlichen Prozessen, künstlerischen Ausdrucksweisen und den Grundfragen menschlicher Existenz zugleich.

Lothar Kittstein

thrilled and fascinated to discover connections with Asia and, in particular, with Chinese culture. As if by itself, *Hair* seeks out places of transition, where things are *no longer* or *not quite* as one expects. It starts out in an empty shell of Europe's once great industrial age and follows the path of Western desire for the Orient with its thick, black hair, mysterious temples and unknown fragrances. From there, it progresses to the socially diverse environment around Cologne's main railway station where, in today's service society, German pub culture blends with the smell of kebabs and the neon lights of the shops selling cheap goods (i.e. plastic toys made in the Far East), and finally ends in the wild undergrowth of the unbridled communist-capitalist growth of Chinese cities which are gradually sucking up and swallowing the villagey world on their fringes. For Hiesl and Kaiser, hair is not a limited issue on which to base an artistic thesis. Rather, *hair* in their work is the key to an artistic investigation of the world in which we live. Just as our hair falls out every day and nestles in the gaps between our furniture, in the fibres of our carpets and in the drains of our shower cabinets, particles of the *hair* issue – thanks to Hiesl and Kaiser's method of working – settle in the most unforeseeable and hidden corners of our daily lives and our cultural consciousness. For the on-looker, any analysis of the phenomenon of hair simultaneously becomes a confrontation with social processes, artistic methods of expression and the basic questions of human existence.

Lothar Kittstein
Translated by Vivien Smith

ZWISCHEN RÄUMEN
Bild und Performance bei Angie Hiesl und Roland Kaiser

In berückenden, enigmatischen Inszenierungen zwischen Performance, Theater, Installation und Bild entfalten Angie Hiesls und Roland Kaisers Choreographien ambivalente Momente zwischen den Gattungen, zwischen öffentlichem und privatem Raum, zwischen Innen und Außen, zwischen Fremdheit und Vertrautheit. In all ihren Projekten entwerfen die Künstler poetische, vieldeutige, in sich gebrochene Erzählstränge, die um Erinnerungen und Verluste, um Intimität und Liebe kreisen. Immer in schwebender Balance geht es dabei auch um die Erkundung von Wahrnehmung im und als Zwischenreich, als kontinuierlicher Prozess, der nie zum Stillstand kommt. Gerade in der Entrückung, in der Überschreitung der alltäglichen Erfahrung des urbanen Raums, die in und von den verrückten, irritierenden tableaux vivants evoziert wird, geschieht wie im Paradox eine Intensivierung unseres Bewusstseins von der – eigenen – Körperlichkeit und unserer unmittelbar gegenwärtigen Existenz: ein Wechselspiel zwischen Entkörperlichung im Bild und Zurückgewinnung des Körpers in der leiblichen Erfahrung der Raumbilder. Und dabei wird auch, fast beiläufig, das so ambivalente Problem aller visuellen Künste verhandelt, das Verhältnis zwischen Präsenz und Repräsentation, zwischen Realem und Fiktivem, zwischen Singularität und Wiederholung, zwischen Kontinuität und inszeniertem Gebilde. In der steten Veränderung der flüchtigen Bilderströme mit ihrem ganz eigenen Rhythmus werden immer neue Aspekte dieser Verhältnisse ausgelotet, wobei in der Überlagerung der Handlungs-, Zeichen- und Sprachebenen, der Gesten, der Atmosphäre des Raums, der Töne, der vergehenden Zeit unausdeutbare und doch luzide bilderzeugende Handlungen in Szene gesetzt werden.

Nicht die Fixierung oder die Übertragung eines Gesehenen steht im Mittelpunkt der Inszenierungen, sondern gerade die Unterhöhlung der Grenzen der Sichtbarkeit in Richtung eines Nie-Gesehenen, einer Abwesenheit. In oszillierender Vielfältigkeit überspannen Hiesls und Kaisers Aufführungen die Barrieren zwischen den Gegensätzen, zwischen Differenz und Distanz formulieren sie eine prekäre Präsenz, eine Passage zu anderen, latenten, imaginierten Bildern, die sich in den gedehnten Augenblicken der Performance entfalten.

Angie Hiesls und Roland Kaisers präzise Improvisationen erzeugen immer eine eigentümliche, unauslotbare Dichte, labile Momente, die auf die veränderbare Ordnung der Dinge antworten, auf das Netz von sich verquickenden Zeitstrukturen der flüchtigen Moderne und ihrer urbanen Landschaften mit ihren Einbrüchen von unbestimmbarem, plötzlichen Kommunikationsüberschuss. Jede Performance lässt ein Feld zwischen Sinnsuche und Sinnverneinung entstehen, wobei die Künstler nicht mehr als Produzenten von Sinn agieren, sondern abge-

THE SPACE BETWEEN
Angie Hiesl and Roland Kaiser – Image and Performance

In mesmerising and enigmatic productions that shift between performance, theatre, installation and image, Angie Hiesl and Roland Kaiser's choreographies unfold moments of ambivalence between the various genres, between public and private space, indoors and outdoors, familiarity and unfamiliarity. In all their projects, the artists create poetic, ambiguous, fractured narrative strands revolving around memories and loss, intimacy and love. And throughout, they also maintain a delicate balance between exploring perception both in and as an intermediate realm, as a continuous process that never comes to a halt.

It is precisely in this shift in reality, in the transcendence of our everyday experience of urban space, which is evoked in and by the distorted, perplexing tableaux vivants, that – paradoxically – the awareness of our own physicality and our immediate, current existence is heightened: it is an interplay between disembodiment in the image and the regaining of the body in the physical experience of the spatial images. And at the same time, almost incidentally, the ambivalent problem that faces all the visual arts is dealt with – the relationship between presence and representation, between the real and the fictive, between singularity and repetition and between continuity and a staged entity. In the constantly changing stream of fleeting images with their very own rhythm ever new aspects of these relationships are fathomed, while in the overlapping levels of action, signs and language, the gestures, the atmosphere of the space, the sounds and the passing time, uninterpretable and yet lucid, image-forming actions are played out.

The focus of the performances is not on specifying or conveying what is seen but rather on undermining the boundaries of the visible and pushing them towards something that has never been seen and which lacks presence. With their oscillating diversity, Hiesl and Kaiser's performances straddle the barriers between opposites, formulating a precarious presence between difference and distance, a passage to other, latent, imagined images that unfold in the extended moments of the performance.

Angie Hiesl and Roland Kaiser's precise improvisations always assume a strange, unfathomable density – moments of uncertainty that respond to the changing order of things, to the network of intertwining temporal structures of fleeting modernity and its urban landscapes, which are interrupted by indefinable, suddenly condensed communication. Each performance creates an area between the search for and the negation of meaning; in the process, the artists no longer act as producers of meaning but are replaced by an anonymous, multivocal choir that is imbued with highly varying attitudes, opinions and vocabulary. In the very different cities and spaces, each choreography

löst werden von einem vielstimmigen, anonymen Chor, in dem sich ganz verschiedene Haltungen, Meinungen, Vokabulare durchdringen. Jede Choreographie schafft in den unterschiedlichsten Städten und Plätzen immer wieder neu einen dynamischen Ort von Ereignissen: Profane Rituale und ein Spiel mit Ausnahme und Regel, mit Sprüngen und Rissen, mit Plötzlichkeiten und Einbrüchen.

Dem Cross-over der Disziplinen, das Angie Hiesls und Roland Kaisers künstlerische Arbeit prägt, korrespondiert dann auch, dass ihre Produktionen selbst grenzüberschreitend agieren, in unterschiedlichen Orten und Kulturen zum Austrag kommen. Die künstlerische Forschung im Zwischenreich zwischen den Bildmedien wird noch einmal um die Facette des interkulturellen Sehens, der Frage nach dem Bild und des Verstehens der Anderen erweitert.

So greift Hiesls und Kaisers transkulturelles Projekt *china-hair-connection Peking-Köln* wagemutig die vielfältigen Bedeutungsschichten des Haares auf – als Symbol, Fetisch, Mythos, Material, soziales und geschlechtliches Zeichen, Transportmittel der Erinnerung, erotisches Signal. In den Performances geschehen suggestive Bilder von irritierender Schönheit. Im Kölner Eigelsteinviertel, hinter dem Hauptbahnhof gelegen, einem Stadtviertel mit engen Straßen, Bahnunterführungen, mit belebten Orten und neuen Unorten, und in Peking im vom Strukturwandel besonders geprägten Stadtteil Caochangdi, zwischen Rohbauten und bereits fertiggestellten Galerieneubauten, an der Grenze zwischen öffentlichem und halböffentlichem Raum. Dabei spielen die Performances mit Wahrnehmung, Irritation von Sehmustern und Clichés. Die sensible Erkundung der Eigenarten, der spezifischen Atmosphäre der urbanen Umgebung gibt den Ausgangspunkt für das interdisziplinäre Ereignis. Das Vorgefundene wird in den künstlerischen Interaktionen präzise eingesetzt. Der Stadtraum wird gleichsam in immer neue Dimensionen getrieben, subtil, skurril, frappierend, fremd, vertraut. Zugleich unternimmt *china-hair-connection Peking-Köln* eine visuelle Recherche von kulturellen Codes, von Besetzungen, Urteilen und Vorurteilen. Jeder Blick auf eine fremde Kultur, jede Reise in ein anderes Land überträgt – notwendigerweise – eigene Erfahrungsstrukturen und Deutungsmuster auf das Andere seiner selbst. Mit der Doppel-Aufführung der Haar-Bilder in Köln und Peking, in zwei so unterschiedlichen Kulturen ist Spiegelung und Selbstbespiegelung und die Begrenztheit methodischer Annäherungen an das Fremde in ein neues Verhältnis gebracht, bleibt unabschließbar, offen, unergründlich.

Wie in der imaginären Reise, die Charles Baudelaire in seinem Gedicht *La Chevelure (Das Haar)* beschreibt, wo das Haar der Geliebten Auslöser für ein unauflösbares Geflecht von Erinnerungsbildern wird, *Erinnerungen, die in diesem Haar schlummern, das schmachtende Asien, das glühende Afrika, eine ganze Welt, sehr weit entlegen, fast gestorben*, verschmelzen

again and again creates a dynamic space with profane rituals and a game with rules and exceptions, with cracks and fissures, with sudden changes and interruptions.

The crossover of disciplines that typifies Angie Hiesl and Roland Kaiser's artistic work also applies to the productions themselves in that they cross borders and are ultimately staged in very different places and cultures. In the intermediate sphere between the visual media the facet of intercultural vision, the questioning of the image and the understanding of others broaden the artistic quest.

Hiesl and Kaiser's transcultural project *china-hair-connection Beijing-Cologne* thus deals boldly with the multifaceted layers of meaning of hair – as a symbol, fetish, myth, material, social and sexual symbol, a means of conveying memory, an erotic signal. Suggestive images of disconcerting beauty occur in the performances: in the Eigelstein district of Cologne behind the city's main rail station, with its narrow streets, railway underpasses, highly frequented spaces and new, non-places, and in Caochangdi, a district of Beijing that is largely characterised by structural change, between shells of buildings and newly built, completed galleries, on the dividing line between public and semi-public space. The performances play with perception, with confused patterns of seeing and with clichés. The sensitive exploration of special features and the specific atmosphere of the urban surroundings provide the starting point for the interdisciplinary event. The existing setting is carefully integrated into the artistic interactions. The urban space is, as it were, propelled into ever-new dimensions – subtle, quirky, striking, alien, familiar. At the same time, *china-hair-connection Beijing-Cologne* conducts visual research into cultural codes, associated meanings, judgements and prejudices. Every glance at a foreign culture, every journey to a foreign country necessarily involves transferring one's structures of experience and patterns of interpretation to the otherness of oneself. Thanks to the two performances of the hair images in two such different cultures – in Cologne and Beijing – reflection, self-reflection and the finiteness of methodical approaches to things foreign enter into a new relationship, and remain inconclusive, open and unfathomable.

As in the imaginary journey that Charles Baudelaire describes in his poem *La Chevelure (Head of Hair)* in which his lover's hair releases an inextricable braid of memory images: *Memories sleeping in that thick head of hair..., Sweltering Africa and languorous Asia, A whole far-away world, absent, almost defunct...*, Hiesl and Kaiser's actions merge disparate layers and facets. The hair motif, transposed into ever new and different situations, reveals its fusing and moving force. These performances shift between cult and culture as if dancing on both sides of the dividing lines, between archaic patterns and rituals and the act of art.

Angie Hiesl and Roland Kaiser's intercultural choreography

Hiesls und Kaisers Aktionen disparate Schichten und Facetten. Das Haar-Motiv, versetzt in je neue und andere Situationen, zeigt sich in seiner amalgamierenden und movierenden Kraft. Es sind Aufführungen zwischen Kult und Kunst, so als ob die Performances auf beiden Seiten der Grenzlinien tanzten, zwischen archaischen Mustern und Riten und dem Ereignis der Kunst.

Angie Hiesls und Roland Kaisers interkulturelle Choreographie thematisiert und unterhöhlt wohl auch die tradierten Vorurteile des *haarigen Europäers*, des glatten adoleszenten Asiaten, die Auffassung des fernen Ostens als erotisch, fremd, geheimnisvoll, leer, mit Menschen ohne eigene Empfindung, gleichförmig und gesichtslos wie die Städte, die ins Endlose wuchern, ohne Tiefgründigkeit, leere Bedeutungsfiguren, bloße Erscheinung. *china-hair-connection Peking-Köln* erprobt Seh- und Erfahrungsmuster, umspielt das Geheimnis und die Wirkung – ganz ohne dörren Vergleich. Als reale Gegenwart ist die ambivalente, lockende Faszination der Haare da, ihre Dauerhaftigkeit und Fragilität, ihr Eigenleben, ihre Zwischenstellung zwischen Natürlichkeit und Künstlichkeit, ihre Struktur, die im Haar gespeicherte Erinnerung.

Haar war immer schon ein Mittel zur Selbstinszenierung, das ein vielfältiges Spiel mit Identität und Identitätswechseln erlaubte. Obwohl immer auch als Ausdrucksträger von Geschlechter- und Rasseidealen instrumentalisiert, ist doch das Haar der Stoff, der die Normierungen des Körpers und festgelegte Rollen umgehen, überspielen kann. Kopfhaare und Körperhaare und das, was wir mit ihnen, aus ihnen und damit aus uns machen – sind etwas Menschliches. Und doch verweisen sie zurück auf unseren Ursprung und die Entwicklung der Arten. Das Haar und der Umgang damit erinnert immer wieder an das Tier in uns, an unsere Naturhaftigkeit. Seine Symbolträchtigkeit, die zentrale Rolle in der Körpersprache und die Vielfalt seiner Bedeutungen scheinen von diesem Doppelcharakter abzuhängen, der sich niemals aufspalten lässt: Auf der einen Seite ist das Haar unauslöschliches Zeichen des Animalischen im Menschen, einschließlich seiner anscheinend überwundenen niederen Triebe. Auf der anderen Seite ist das Haar kulturell festgelegtes Kultiviertheitsmaß, Zeichen, Symbol. Im Schneiden, Waschen, Färben, Formen, Rasieren, in all dem, was schließlich die Frisur und die Körperbehaarung ausmacht, gestalten wir, was uns wichtig scheint, und preisen es der Mitwelt an. Frisieren, Rasieren wird so gesehen zu einer Form des Mitteilens, der Kommunikation, der Selbstdarstellung – kein Wunder, dass Haar als Material in der Kunst des 20. Jahrhunderts vielfach zum Einsatz kommt.

Schon eine Passage aus Luis Buñuels Erinnerungen *Mein letzter Seufzer* beschreibt ein halluzinatorisches Erlebnis: Auf der Suche nach Abenteuern im Labyrinth der Straßen des nächtlichen Madrids trifft er mit einer Gruppe von Freunden auf einen blinden Mann, der die Gruppe mit nach Hause nimmt, in

broaches and indeed also undermines prejudices that have been handed down through the ages: the stereotype of the *hairy European*, the smoothly adolescent Asian or the perception of the Far East as erotic, foreign, mysterious, empty, inhabited by people without individual feelings, people as uniform and faceless as the endlessly sprawling cities, people lacking in depth – empty, meaningless symbols, mere apparitions. *china-hair-connection Beijing-Cologne* tests patterns of seeing and experience; it revolves around mystery and its effect – without making cut-and-dried comparisons. The ambivalent, enticing fascination of hair is there as a real presence, with its durability and fragility, its own life, its intermediate position between naturalness and artificiality, its structure and the memories that are stored in hair.

Hair has always been a means of self-presentation, enabling one to play games with identity and changes in identity in a variety of ways. While it has always also been exploited to express ideals of gender and race, hair is after all the stuff that eschews or glosses over the standardisation of the body and defined roles. Head hair, body hair and what we do with it – and thus what we make of ourselves – is human. And yet hair is a throwback to our origins and the evolution of the species. Hair and the way we handle it always reminds us of the animal in us, of our natural origins. Its symbolism, the central role it plays in body language and the range of interpretations it permits seem to depend upon its dual nature, which can never be divided. On the one hand, hair is an indelible sign of the animal in man, including the base instincts that we have apparently overcome. On the other hand, hair serves as a culturally defined benchmark of sophistication, as a sign, a symbol. When we cut, wash, colour, style or shave our hair, in other words in everything we do to create a hairstyle or style our body hair, we shape what seems important to us and show it off to those around us. In that sense, hairstyling and shaving become a form of conveying information, of communication and self-expression. No wonder, then, that hair is often used as a material in the art of the 20th century.

A passage in Luis Buñuel's memoirs *My Last Sigh* describes a hallucinatory experience. Out at night with a group of friends in search of adventure in the labyrinth of Madrid's streets, Buñuel meets a blind man, who takes the group back to his house, to rooms without light sources, but instead with pictures and objects made entirely of hair – *trenches made of hair, cypresses made of hair*. This surrealist anecdote may indicate the increasing crossing of material borders and the use of unorthodox and unusual materials in 20th century art, which implies a disruption or shake-up of the traditional theory of art, in which beauty was always regarded as an expression of order, while hair was threatening. For Winckelmann or Herder, for example, any sculpture was considered defaced if a single hair (apart from hair on the head or eyebrows) was evident

Räume ohne Lichtquellen, dafür mit Bildern und Objekten, die ganz aus Haaren gemacht waren, *Gräben aus Haaren, Zypressen aus Haaren*. Diese surrealistische Anekdote mag ein Hinweis auf die zunehmenden materialen Grenzüberschreitungen, auf den Einsatz von unorthodoxen und ungewöhnlichen Materialien in der Kunst des 20. Jahrhunderts sein, der eine Störung oder Aufstörung der klassischen Kunsttheorie beinhaltet, für die Schönheit immer auch ein Ordnungsbegriff war und Haar eine Bedrohung. Für Winckelmann oder Herder beispielsweise galt jede Skulptur als verunstaltet, wenn sich (außer dem Haupthaar und den Brauen) nur ein winziges Härchen auf der makellosen weißen Oberfläche der Plastik zeigte. Mit Herders Worten war das Haar ein Schauer, eine Scharte, etwas, das die Form hindert, nicht zu ihr gehört. All diese vielschichtigen, vielfältigen Konnotationen des Stoffes Haar sind in Angie Hiesls und Roland Kaisers Hair-Connection da, verflechten sich, lösen sich in einer Rebusfolge (Rebus = durch die Dinge) aus Bildern und Zeichen, verstörend, luzide, subversiv und kühn.

Die Fragen nach Identität und Ort greifen auch die szenischen Aktionen, die bildnerischen Installationen von *ZWILLINGE - how do I know I am me ...* (Uraufführung 2001, Köln) auf. In einer Form, die zwischen Aufführung und Ausstellung changiert, inszenieren Hiesl und Kaiser den prekären Status der Zwillingsexistenz, die in fast allen Kulturen zu symbolischer Deutung, sei es im positiven oder im negativen Sinn, Anlass gegeben hat: Doppelwesen, Doppelgänger, Zwillinge gelten – trotz ihrer zunehmenden Häufigkeit – immer noch als etwas Besonderes, Außergewöhnliches, wenn nicht Fragwürdiges. Das vitale Thema von Gleichheit und Verschiedenheit, der beunruhigende Aspekt, das zwei sozusagen eins sind, sind in solche Interpretationen eingelagert. Mythen, Erzählungen, Forschungen umkreisen das Zwillingsphänomen in aller Ambivalenz. Zwillingen hat man besondere Kräfte zugemessen, manche Kulturen haben sie als Gottheiten verehrt, andererseits wird ihnen mitunter auch etwas Bedrohliches und Gefährliches unterstellt. Angie Hiesls und Roland Kaisers Dramaturgie greift diese Vielschichtigkeit des Zwillingsthemas auf, treibt es in ihren Bildern in ein Vexierspiel von Spiegelbildlichkeit, Täuschung, Verwechslung, Verdoppelung, Vereinzelung – das Wunder in der Ordnung der Natur wird dabei nicht entschlüsselt, sondern in einem Panorama, das Theater, Performance, Klang, Bild und den Ort der Aufführung miteinander verwebt, als andauerndes, doppelbödiges Faszinosum entfaltet.

Nach einer Definition des amerikanischen Soziologen Richard Sennett ist die Stadt der Ort, in der die Wahrscheinlichkeit besteht, dass Fremde sich begegnen. Der urbane Raum ist zugleich ein Ort von Lust und Gefahr, von Chance und Bedrohung, in dem Flaneure, Touristen, Spieler unterwegs sind, mit einer ganz spezifischen Weise des Zusammentreffens, ohne Vergangenheit, ohne Geschichte, ohne Zukunft – hier verwan-

on the flawless white surface of the sculpture. To use Herder's words, hair was frightful, a blemish, something that obstructed the form and did not belong to it. All these multilayered, diverse connotations of hair as a material are present in Angie Hiesl and Roland Kaiser's hair-connection. They intertwine with one another, then disentangle themselves in a succession of rebus pictures and symbols that are unsettling, lucid, subversive and bold.

The staged actions, the artistic installations of *TWINS - how do I know I am me ...* (premiered in Cologne in 2001) also address the issue of identity and space. In a form that shifts between performance and exhibition, Hiesl and Kaiser present the precarious status of life as a twin, which in almost all cultures has assumed a symbolic meaning, whether in a positive or negative sense: dual beings, doppelgangers, twins — despite their increasing frequency — are always considered to be something special and extraordinary, if not questionable.

The vital subject of sameness and difference, the disconcerting aspect that two are one, so to speak, is embedded in such interpretations. Myths, stories and research revolve around the phenomenon of twins in all its ambivalence. Special powers are ascribed to twins, and some cultures revere them as deities, while on the other hand they are also believed to be somehow threatening and dangerous. Angie Hiesl and Roland Kaiser's dramaturgy deals with the complexity of the twins theme and the images which they use propel it into a puzzle based on mirror images, illusion, confusion, duplication and isolation. In the process, the miracle of the order of nature is not decoded but unfurls in a panorama that interweaves theatre, performance, sound, image and the performance venue as a lasting, ambiguous fascination.

The American sociologist Richard Sennett once defined the city as a place where strangers meet. Urban space is at the same time a setting for desire and danger, for chance and menace, a place where flaneurs, tourists and players are out and about. It permits a very specific type of encounter, without a past, without history, without a future. Here strangers are transformed into surfaces without anything before or behind them. The modern city with its multiple layers of othernesses repeatedly becomes the setting for Hiesl and Kaiser's performance actions – and this strange life of others that passes by pedestrians as they walk through cities is then once again alienated and heightened in new, never-before-seen configurations of performers and objects that are integrated into the action. The curious nature of city encounters that do not obliterate but rather heighten the strangeness of strangers is, perhaps, a concentration of these enigmatic episodes that Hiesl and Kaiser bring into their work, in the carefully arranged events that deal with this strangeness yet familiarity, proximity yet distance – in all their ambivalence. The performance *x-times people chair* (premiered in Cologne in 1995) is also staged in

deln sich die Fremden in Oberflächen, ohne Davor oder Dahinter. Die moderne Stadt mit ihren vielfach gestaffelten Andersheiten wird für Angie Hiesls und Roland Kaisers performative Aktionen immer wieder zum Schauplatz, und dieses merkwürdige Leben der Anderen, das bei Spaziergängen durch die Städte an den Passanten vorbeizieht, wird dann noch einmal verfremdet, in neuen, nie gesehenen Anordnungen von handelnden Akteuren und mitspielenden Objekten gesteigert. Die eigenartige Natur der Stadtbegegnungen, die die Fremdheit der Fremden ja nicht tilgen, sondern eher verstärken, ist vielleicht das Konzentrat dieser enigmatischen Episoden, die Hiesl und Kaiser ins Werk setzen, in den sorgfältig arrangierten Ereignissen, die mit dieser Fremd-Vertrautheit, Nah-Ferne umgehen – in aller Ambivalenz. In verschiedenen Städten in Europa und Südamerika spielt so auch die Aktions-Installation *x-mal Mensch Stuhl* (Uraufführung 1995, Köln).

Häuserfassaden an Straßen und Plätzen im urbanen Raum werden zum Bildgrund, wenn diese Fassaden in einer Höhe zwischen drei und sieben Metern mit weißen, schlichten Stahlstühlen bestückt werden. Auf ihnen sitzen, hoch über den Köpfen der Passanten, Menschen im Alter von sechzig bis weit über siebzig. Und diese Menschen auf Stühlen führen – ihrem normalen Standpunkt, ihrem Ort und der Wahrnehmungsperspektive des Betrachters ganz entrückt – doch sehr alltägliche, auf fast beiläufige Weise inszenierte Handlungen aus: Sie lesen in einer Zeitung, sie schneiden Brot oder legen Wäsche zusammen. Es sind völlig unspektakuläre Tätigkeiten, die mit ihrem (und unserem) Alltagsleben in Verbindung stehen. Die rätselhaften, wunderbaren Bilder verschränken sich mit Einbrüchen eines (ungewissen) Realen – und vice versa, das Alltäglichwirkliche (und sein versteckter Reichtum) wird zu einem Feld von wundersamen Ereignissen. Aktionen und Handlungen im realen Zeit-Raum kippen ins Bild, werden Kunstwerk, auf und mit dem Leib geschriebene Körperbilder, im Zwischenraum zwischen faktischem Tun, Improvisation und inszenierter Choreographie: ein mobiles und mobilisierendes Verfahren, das sich immer in dynamische Spannung zu der Umgebung, zu Seherwartungen und Sehstandards setzt. Die bewegende und bewegliche Energie der Inszenierungen liegt in der uneinholbaren Prozessualität des Sehens als einem unkalkulierbaren Gleiten zwischen einem *Hier* und einem *Nirgendwo*, zwischen einem Fassbaren und einem Unausschöpflichen, zwischen den agierenden Personen, den Dingen, und ihren Schatten: das unabschließbare Potential, die Freiheit der Kunst.

War die belebte Stadt die Bühne für *x-mal Mensch Stuhl*, so spielt die Performance MAKADAM (Uraufführung 2007, Köln) gleichsam auf der anderen Seite der modernen Städte, an dem Un-Ort einer Industriebrache, die eigentlich jeden Gedanken an ein Verweilen verbietet, in einem Raum, in dem die Gegenwart Ausdruck und Sinn zerstört hat. Aus Ödland wird Aktionsfläche, umgemünzt und neu definiert durch die Handlungen

various cities in Europe and South America. House facades in streets and squares in urban spaces create the background against which simple white chairs are attached at a height of three to seven metres above the ground. Seated on them, high up above the heads of passers-by, are men and women aged from 60 to well over 70. These people on chairs, who are far removed from their normal standpoint and location and from the perspective of the onlooker, perform everyday actions, almost incidentally, such as reading a newspaper, slicing bread or folding laundry. These are completely unspectacular activities connected with their and our daily lives. The wonderful, puzzling images are interlaced with sudden insights into an uncertain reality – and vice versa, the everyday reality (with its hidden riches) becomes an area filled with wonderful events. Actions and activities in real timespace shift into the image and become a work of art with images that are exactly tailored to and moulded with bodies in the space between the actual activity, improvisation and staged choreography: a mobile and mobilising procedure that always creates a dynamic tension with the surroundings, with visual expectations and visual standards. The moving, flexible energy of the performances lies in the unattainable processuality of seeing as an incalculable gliding between *here* and *nowhere*, between the comprehensible and the inexhaustible, between the performers, the objects and their shadows: the infinite potential, the freedom of art.

While a busy city was the stage for *x-times people chair*, MACADAM (premiered in Cologne in 2007) is performed on the other side of modern cities, in the non-space of an industrial wasteland, where one would never wish to linger, in a space where the present has destroyed all expression and meaning. Wasteland becomes a platform for action, converted and redefined by the actions of the performers who are stranded in no-man's land. Their ghostly presence in such a leftover place unfurls itself surprisingly in off-beat scenes between structured form and the chaos of the world.

The implanted artefacts – a telephone box, toy cars, a laid table in the midst of this desolate space, a piece of asphalt, which leads back to the title of the performance – thus become familiar yet unfamiliar materials, fellow players of the performers in this wasteland.

Boundary crossings and borderline experiences occur again and again in Angie Hiesl and Roland Kaiser's productions – and in ever new forms. The flood of images they instil in their work, which masterfully circumnavigate the predictable and mask simple causality, make reality porous and open up an imaginary sphere. Images appear, embedded in their context, and yet step out of it. Ultimately, their work is also always about what lurks behind us, about chasms and cracks that open up and suddenly transpose the viewer into another sphere.

Dorothée Bauerle-Willert
Translated by Vanessa Anderson

der im Niemandsland gestrandeten Performer. Ihre geisterhafte Präsenz in einem solchen, wie übriggebliebenen Ort entrollt sich überraschend in schrägen Akten, zwischen strukturierter Gestalt und dem Chaos der Welt.

Die implantierten Artefakte, eine Telefonzelle, Spielzeugautos, ein auf der öden Fläche gedeckter Tisch, ein Stück Asphalt, das zum Titel der Performance zurückführt, sind dann wie fremdvertraute Materialien, Mitspieler der Akteure im Brachland. In Angie Hiesls und Roland Kaisers Produktionen geschehen – immer wieder und immer wieder neu – Überschreitungen und Grenzerfahrungen. Die von ihnen ins Werk gesetzten Bilderfluten, die Vorhersehbares souverän umschiffen und simple Kausalität ausblenden, machen die Wirklichkeit porös, öffnen einen Platz des Imaginären. Bilder tauchen auf, sie haben ihren Ort in ihrem Kontext und treten doch aus ihm heraus: immer geht es auch um das, was im Rücken bleibt, um Abgründe und Risse, die jäh ins Andere versetzen.

Dorothée Bauerle-Willert

china-hair-connection
beijing-cologne
part one: cologne

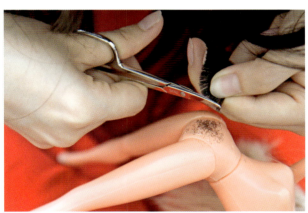

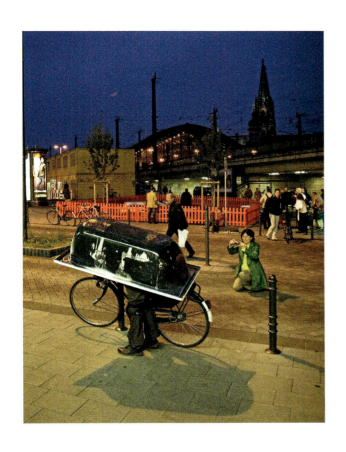

我说我爱你，
为什么自由

I say I love you, but you sa
Why is freedom mor

你说你要自由。
比爱更重要？

ou want to have freedom.
mportant than love? ...

A Concise Chinese-English Dictionary For Lovers
by Guo Xiaolu, London: Vintage, 2008

china-hair-connection beijing-cologne

part two: beijing

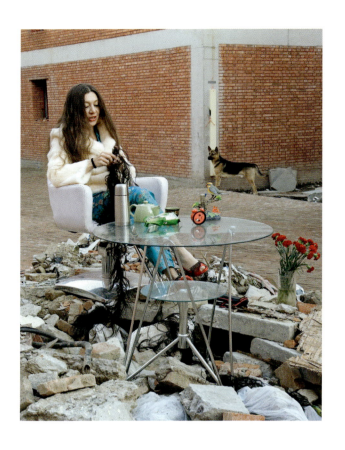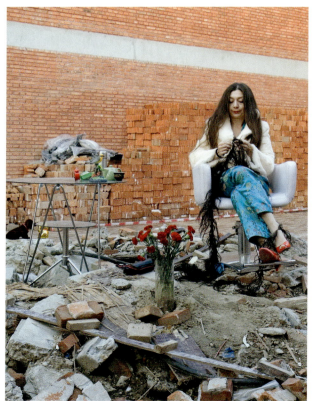

Das Projekt *china-hair-connection* Peking-Köln: Eine Fallstudie in interkultureller Zusammenarbeit

Wie alles begann

Die Basis für das *china-hair-connection* Projekt wurde im Frühjahr 2005 gelegt, als Angie Hiesl und Roland Kaiser von Borneoco und dem Living Dance Studio (LDS) eingeladen worden waren, einen Workshop in der Caochangdi Workstation zu leiten und durchzuführen, dem funkelnagelneuen, unabhängigen Zentrum des LDS für darstellende Künste in Peking. In diesem Workshop stellten Hiesl und Kaiser ihre Themen und ihre Art von ortspezifischem Arbeiten vor, was für viele der Workshop-TeilnehmerInnen manch überraschende und neue Sichtweisen eröffnete. Einige von ihnen wurden dadurch für immer zu treuen Fans von Angie und Roland! Die Zuneigung war gegenseitig: China und seine PerformerInnen bekamen einen bleibenden Eindruck von Angie und Roland, die ihrerseits davon träumten, dort zu leben und zu arbeiten.

Das *china-hair-connection* Projekt hat viele Aspekte der interkulturellen Arbeit berührt — zu viele, um sie hier im Einzelnen darzustellen. Aber einige interessante Aspekte haben sich in unsere Erinnerung als wirklich bemerkenswert und interessant eingeprägt.

Als ortspezifische Arbeit hat sich das *china-hair-connection* Projekt unterschiedlichen Herausforderungen in Deutschland und China gestellt. Öffentlicher Raum in China (besonders in Peking im Jahr der Olympischen Spiele!) ist eher staatlicher Raum als öffentlicher Raum. So wurde der öffentliche Raum des Eigelstein in Köln zu einem halböffentlichen Raum in China: ein Innenhof mit vielen Kunstgalerien und der daran vorbeiführenden Straße.

Aber welch ungewöhnliche Wirkung hatte diese Performance an diesem halbabgeschiedenen Ort! Die chinesischen Wanderarbeiter, die in der Nachbarschaft wohnten, hatten diesen Ort oder die Galerien im Inneren noch nie betreten. Aber jetzt, neugierig gemacht durch einige kurze Einblicke in die Performance auf der Mauer oder auf der Straße, strömten diese Menschen in den Hof und schauten der Aufführung stundenlang intensiv zu. Bei der zweiten und dritten Aufführung beteiligten sich Leute aus dem Publikum, insbesondere Kinder an der Performance, spielten mit einigen der Objekte oder assistierten manchmal den Schauspielern, was zu dem Paradox führte, dass in diesem halböffentlichen Raum wahrscheinlich mehr Menschen ihre erste Einführung in die ortspezifische Performance-Kunst bekamen als in dem öffentlichen Raum in Köln.

china-hair-connection Beijing-Cologne: A case study in cross cultural collaboration

How it started

The basis for *china-hair-connection Beijing-Cologne* was laid in spring 2005, when Borneoco and Living Dance Studio (LDS) invited Angie Hiesl and Roland Kaiser to conduct a workshop in Caochangdi Workstation, LDS's brand new centre for independent performing arts in Beijing. In this workshop Hiesl and Kaiser introduced their way of working site-specifically and their themes — a true eye-opener for many of the workshop participants. Some of them became eternal fans of Angie and Roland! The love was reciprocal: China and its performers got a firm hold on Angie and Roland, who dreamed of working and living there.

china-hair-connection touched upon many aspects of working across cultures — too many to discuss in great detail here. But a few interesting aspects have stuck in our minds as truly remarkable or interesting.

As a site-specific work, *china-hair-connection* met different challenges in Germany and in China. Public space in China (especially in Beijing in the year of the Olympics!) is more government space than public space. So the public space of Cologne Eigelstein became a semi-public space in China: a courtyard with many art galleries and the surrounding road.

But what a remarkable effect the performance in this semi-secluded area had! The Chinese migrants living in the neighbourhood had never entered this area or the galleries inside before. But now these people, attracted by a few glimpses of the performance on the wall or the road, flocked into the yard and spent hours intensely watching the performance.
The second and third performance had the audience, especially children, joining in, playing with some of the objects or assisting some of the actors and leading to the paradox that in this semi-public space probably more people got their first introduction to site-specific performance art than in the public space in Cologne.

Während das entspannte und gemächliche Tempo des *china-hair-connection* Projektes einerseits sehr gut zur Neugierde der Chinesen und ihrer Liebe zu langsamen, ausgedehnten Aufführungen gepasst hat, ist es andererseits auch ein Aufeinandertreffen von Gegensätzen zwischen den deutschen Meistern der Detailgenauigkeit (Angie und Roland) und den chinesischen Meistern der Improvisation (das Living Dance Studio) gewesen. Für Angie und Roland beinhaltete das *china-hair-connection Peking-Köln* Projekt ein sehr ins Detail gehendes, genaues Arbeiten, das eine vorausschauende Planung erforderte. Für die chinesischen Künstler der freien Szene ist Vorausplanung oft eine Zeitverschwendung, weil man nicht wissen kann, wie die Situation in der nächsten Woche, im nächsten Monat oder gar im nächsten Jahr sein wird. Jahre des Arbeitens und Lebens unter ungewissen Bedingungen hat sie bestens dafür qualifiziert, Dinge erst im letzten Augenblick zu regeln und zu tun. Nicht immer einfach für Europäer!

Das *china-hair-connection* Projekt mit seinen Debatten über die Symbolik, die sich mit dem Thema *Haar* in China und Deutschland verbindet, mit seinen chinesischen PerformerInnen, die vorher noch nie im öffentlichen Raum aufgetreten sind, mit seinen sehr praktischen Problemen, einen Gebrauchtwagen in China zu finden, mit seinen Dilemmas, ob man zum Beispiel Barbiepuppen mit oder ohne Schamhaar in China verwenden sollte, all dies war nicht immer einfach, aber es war eine bereichernde Erfahrung, sowohl für die Teilnehmer als auch die Zuschauer!

Dineke Koerts und Constance Vos
Übersetzung von Richard Volk

Whereas the leisurely pace of *china-hair-connection* matched very well the Chinese curiosity and love of slow, extended performances, the project was also a confrontation between the German Masters of Detail (Angie and Roland) and the Chinese Masters of Improvisation (the Living Dance Studio). For Angie and Roland, *china-hair-connection Beijing-Cologne* meant very detailed and precise work that required planning ahead. For Chinese independent artists planning ahead is often a waste of time as they never know what the situation will be next week, next month, let alone next year. Years of working and living in uncertain conditions have made them experts in doing things at a late stage. Not always easy for Europeans!

china-hair-connection Beijing-Cologne with its discussions about the symbolism connected to hair in China and Germany, with its Chinese performers never having performed in public space before, with its very practical problems of how to find a used car in China, with its dilemmas like yes or no pubic hair on Barbie dolls in China, was not always easy but an enriching experience for participants and audience alike!

Dineke Koerts and Constance Vos

HAAR OHNE SUPPE
Beeindruckende Kunstaktion in Caochangdi

china-hair-connection Beijing-Cologne, das ist der Titel eines interdisziplinären Performance-Projekts im öffentlichen Raum von Angie Hiesl und Roland Kaiser. Ende August waren sieben chinesische und vier europäische Performer und Performerinnen im Kölner Eigelstein-Viertel zu Gast. Mitte September siedelte sich die Produktion in Beijing an, um dort bis Mitte Oktober eine ortsbezogene Variation von *china-hair-connection Beijing-Cologne* zu erarbeiten und aufzuführen.

...

Man zog mit den reichhaltigen Requisiten nach Caochangdi, dem Gräserfeld und alten Weidegebiet der Rösser des Qing-Kaiserhofs weit außerhalb der damaligen Hauptstadt. Heute liegt das Gebiet allerdings gleich hinter dem Fünften Ring, nicht weit von der Kunstmeile 798 entfernt. Anders als die Kunstmeile, die mittlerweile in rasanter Geschwindigkeit Kommerzialisierung und Banalisierung erlebt, steht Caochangdi noch am Anfang seiner Umwandlung. Ländlich, noch nicht einmal vorstädtisch ist der Charakter des Ortes. In Dashanzi, wo 798 liegt, standen bereits seit den 50er Jahren Fabrikgebäude, die nun zu Galerien und Cafés transformiert sind, während hier nur Felder und Weiden waren.

Die Kunstmacher und -händler, die sich nun ansiedeln, bauen neu: Ziegelhäuser, die stilistisch zwischen Hutong und Bauhaus Dessau stehen, wie das Haus eines frühen Entdeckers des Ortes, Ai Weiwei, Kunstfex und Mitgestalter des Olympiastadions *Vogelnest*.

...

Haar verbindet
Die Hair Connection machte also ein Areal inmitten von Caochangdi zum Schauplatz ihrer Performance, ein Areal, das gerade fertiggestellt ist: zwei bis dreistöckige Gebäude, die aussehen, als stammten sie aus einem Gemälde von Giorgio de Chirico. Zwischen ihnen klinkersteingepflasterte Straßen, Wege und Plätze, teils noch unvollendet. Galerien sind bislang nur vereinzelt eingezogen, Bauschutt und Baumaterial unterstreichen das Vorläufige der Szenerie. In der Nachbarschaft, einige Ecken weiter, ist auch die Workstation des Living Dance Studio Beijing der Choreographin Wen Hui und des Dokumentarfilmers Wu Wenguang, aus dem die chinesischen Teilnehmer des Projektes stammen.

...

Die metaphysischen Straßenzüge des Kunstareals kreuzen auch die bodenständig den Alltag seiner Menschen durchziehende Hauptstraße des Dorfes. Dadurch konnte es einströmen, das unbearbeitete Leben, des Künstlers Rohstoff vor jener Stilisierung, die dann in der Performance zu besichtigen war. Und die Menschen, gerade auch die nicht extra angereisten, die von

HAIR WITHOUT SOUP
Impressive performance art in Caochangdi

china-hair-connection Beijing-Cologne is an interdisciplinary project by Angie Hiesl and Roland Kaiser performed in public space. At the end of August, seven Chinese and four European performers made guest appearances in Cologne's Eigelstein district. In mid-September, the production moved to Beijing, where the team worked until mid-October on a site-specific version of *china-hair-connection Beijing-Cologne* which they then performed.

...

The company took along a rich assortment of props to Caochangdi, a former grazing area for horses of the Qing imperial court far outside the former capital. Today, however, the area lies directly beyond the Fifth Ring Road, not far from the 798 Art Zone. In contrast to this zone, which is now rapidly falling prey to commercialization and banality, Caochangdi is in the early stages of transition. Still rural in character, it has not yet assumed any of the features of suburbanization. Dashanzi, where 798 is located, has been home to factory buildings since the 1950s. These are now being turned into galleries and cafés, where once there were only fields and pastureland.

The art makers and dealers relocating here are starting from scratch: new brick buildings are going up which, in terms of style, fit somewhere between Hutong and the Bauhaus in Dessau. A good example is the house of Ai Weiwei, artist and co-designer of the *Bird's Nest* Olympic Stadium, and one of the first people to discover this place.

...

Hair bonds
Hair Connection made an area in the center of Caochangdi the setting for the performance. This area has just been completed with two to three-story buildings that look like something out of a painting by Giorgio de Chirico. Between them are cobblestone streets, paths and squares, some of them still unfinished. To date, only a few galleries have moved in. Rubble and building materials underscore the temporary nature of the surroundings. In the same neighborhood, just a few blocks further along, is the Living Dance Studio Beijing. Run by choreographer Wen Hui and documentary filmmaker Wu Wenguang, this is the studio from where the Chinese participants in the project come.

...

The metaphysical streets of the Art Zone also criss-cross the down-to-earth main street of Caochangdi village abuzz with people going about their daily lives. It provided the unprocessed life – the artist's raw material – that was then stylized and became visible in the performance. The onlookers – particularly those who had not travelled here specially – enjoyed watching

der Dorfstraße, haben es genossen, der deutsch-chinesischen Choreographie zuzuschauen. Die bewegte sich zwischen der zeremonialen Würde einer Springprozession und der ironischen Schulterung des schweren kulturgeschichtlichen Gepäcks, das wir normalerweise auf dem Kopf tragen, gleich, ob sich dort noch Haare befinden oder das nicht minder gravitätische Symbol ihrer spiegelblanken Abwesenheit. Neueste Forschungen wollen herausgefunden haben, dass bereits vor 200 000 Jahren Haupthaar ein Merkmal sozialen Status gewesen ist, weil für eine angemessene Pflege beeindruckender Frisuren die Hilfe vieler Mitprimaten erforderlich war.

Haarkult – Haarkultur

Haar, das ist Anspielung und Konkretum in allen Kulturen. Sitz von Kraft, Stolz und Würde. Objekt der Magie: wer Haare eines Menschen erwirbt, kann damit Liebes- und Schadenszauber betreiben. Die Art, wie Haar getragen wird, unterliegt der Mode und dem Reglement der Gruppen einer Gesellschaft. Frisur kann oktroyiert werden: wie der Zopf, den erst die Mandschu den bezwungenen Chinesen unter Androhung der Todesstrafe auferlegten, der im Abendland aber jahrhundertlang als klassisches Merkmal des Chinamannes galt. Das Abschneiden des Zopfes wurde am Ende der Qing-Dynastie zu einer lebensgefährlichen Geste politischen Aufbegehrens und ein nicht nur symbolischer Schritt auf dem Weg in die Moderne. Heute ist China neben Indien der größte Lieferant für menschliches Haar, nicht nur für die Perückenmacher der Welt, sondern auch für die Chemieindustrie, die aus dem Keratin der Haare Backmittel macht. Wie früher in Europa das Handwerk der Bader und Badstübner mit der Prostitution assoziiert wurde, firmieren heute in chinesischen Städten Huren oft unter dem Zeichen des Friseurhandwerks.

Die einzelnen Stationen der *hair connection* sind von großer Schönheit und stecken voll unentzifferbarer Chiffren. Das aber stößt den Zuschauer nicht ab, sondern zieht ihn nur noch tiefer hinein in jene Mischung aus Körper- und Seelenkult, die sich vor seinen Augen ausbreitet. Ein Kult, den man gut ertragen kann, da er trotz des Ernstes der Tänzer ironisiert wird durch die burlesken Details der Requisiten und Aktionen. Die Darsteller sind stets mit sich selbst, Eigen- und Fremdhaar oder einer Requisite beschäftigt. Lediglich in einer einzigen Szene nehmen sie Kontakt miteinander auf: aber auch das geschieht nur, um einen Protagonisten, der sich als Sperrgut in einem Koffer breitgemacht hat, aus der Szene zu führen.

Barbarische Barbie

Barbiepuppen, deren wesentliches Geschlechtsmerkmal seit fünfzig Jahren überlange Haare sind, weil die Mädchen, die sie besitzen, davon träumen, Pferdepflegerin oder Friseuse zu werden, hatten in Caochangdi teils ihre Köpfe eingebüßt: der

the Sino-German choreography. It shifted between the ceremonial grandeur of a Roman Catholic dancing procession and the ironic shouldering of the heavy art historical baggage that we normally carry on our heads, regardless of whether they are still covered by hair or by the no less illustrious symbol of its shining absence. Latest research suggests that even 200,000 years ago hair was a symbol of social status because the help of numerous fellow primates was needed in order to maintain impressive hairstyles.

Hair cult – Hair culture

In all cultures, hair is both an allusion and a tangible reality. It is the root of strength, pride and dignity. It has magical powers; anyone who obtains another person's hair can weave a love spell or cast an evil spell. Fashion – and social groupings – dictate how hair is worn. A hairstyle can also be imposed – like the pigtail, which the Manchu forced the Chinese to wear under threat of the death penalty. For centuries, the West regarded it as a classic feature of a Chinaman. Cutting off the pigtail became a life-endangering gesture of political rebellion at the end of the Qing dynasty and not just a mere symbolic step into the modern world. Today China is second only to India as the biggest supplier of human hair, not only for the world's wigmakers but also for the chemical industry, which makes baking agents from the keratin contained in hair. As in earlier times in Europe, the barber's and barber surgeon's trade was associated with prostitution. In contemporary Chinese cities, prostitutes often ply their trade in barber shops.

The individual stations in *Hair Connection* are extremely beautiful and are full of indecipherable numbers. But that does not deter the onlookers. Instead it draws them even deeper into the blend of body-and-soul cult extending before their very eyes. It is easy to tolerate because despite their earnestness, the dancers use the burlesque details of the props and actions to poke fun at it. The performers are always occupied with themselves, with their own hair, with someone else's hair or with a prop. In only one scene do they establish contact with each other. And that only happens in order to remove from the scene a protagonist who has slumped awkwardly in a suitcase.

Barbaric Barbie

Barbie Dolls have existed for 50 years. With their extra-long hair, they feed the dreams of their young owners that they will one day become a horse groom or a hairdresser. In Caochangdi some of the Barbie dolls had lost their heads. The neck joint onto which the plastic head would normally have been fixed was transformed by a mesh of little plaits into a sort of bollard, enabling young girls to *anchor* their dreams of hair care and hairdressing without having to make a detour over Barbie's never-changing, permanently grinning face.

Halszapfen, der Wulst, auf dem ihnen sonst die Plastikköpfchen aufgesteckt sind, war hier durch die Schlinge kleiner Zöpfchen in einen Poller verwandelt, an dem der Mädchentraum von Haarpflege und Coiffeur-Handwerk andocken kann, ohne den Umweg über das Grinsen des immer gleichen Barbiegesichtes zu nehmen.

Andere Barbies durften ihren Kopf aufbehalten und in einem gläsernen Regal posieren. Ungleich ihrer Schwestern aus der Serienproduktion fehlten ihnen die Schamhaare nicht. Haar als Erotikum, die Locken der Geliebten und das zum Zopf geflochtene goldene Haar als Kletterhilfe in das Schlafzimmer. Eine Tänzerin wischte mit ihren Haaren die Fenster der Absteige der Barbie-Clone. Die mochten sich alle im Jahre 2002 für das Casting beworben haben zu jenem Animationsfilm, in dem Rapunzel von Barbie verkörpert wurde, und damit auf märchenhafte Weise die behauptete Geschlechtslosigkeit der Barbie-Welt ad absurdum führte.

Wackeldackel meets Winkekatze
Auf dem Schutthaufen eines Hotelzimmers, ich nenne es *Hotel Abgrund* oder die alte Kaiserstadt Hué, nachdem sie zum Kampfgebiet erklärt worden war, sitzt eine Frau und strickt einen Schal aus Haar. Sie rezitiert Bruchstücke aus dem *A Concise Chinese-English Dictionary For Lovers* der Guo Xiaolu. Der Roman spielt in London und beschreibt die éducation sentimentale einer jungen Chinesin vom Lande. Es ist ein Vademecum für alle, die der Sprachlosigkeit der Liebe aufhelfen wollen im west-östlichen Dialog.

Zu ihren Füße eine Winkekatze, Maneki Neko, volkstümliches japanisches Glückssymbol, jetzt auch in China populär, in dieser Ausführung golden, ein Symbol für Reichtum, ihr linker Arm winkt, Zeichen für das Anlocken vieler Menschen. Ihr gegenüber sitzt der gute deutsche Wackeldackel, der seinen Kopf ununterscheidbar in Zustimmung oder Ablehnung oder auch nur im Rhythmus des Windes schüttelt. Das sind zwei, die sich anschmachten, aber ihr Fellhaar ist zu kurz, als dass sich eine Verbindung herstellen ließe. Und so winken sie und wackeln sie, bis sie am Ende der Performance wieder in die dunkle Schachtel des Requisiteurs gesteckt werden und die Reise im Container nach Europa antreten.

Matthias Mersch
Auszug aus *Beijing Rundschau*,
die deutschsprachige Ausgabe
des Wochenmagazins *Beijing Review,* 21-11-2008

Other Barbies in the performance were allowed to keep their heads and pose in a glass cabinet. Unlike their mass-produced sisters, they had pubic hair. Hair as an erotic feature, the locks of a lover and golden hair plaited to make a rope that can be climbed – up to the bedroom. One dancer used her hair to wipe the windows of the Barbie clones' hangout. Any of them could have auditioned for the 2002 animated film in which Barbie played Rapunzel, taking the sexlessness of the Barbie world to absurd limits in fairy tale style.

Nodding dog meets beckoning cat
In the wreckage of a hotel room – let me call it the *Abyss Hotel* or the old imperial city of Hué after it was declared a combat zone – a woman sits knitting hair into a scarf. She is reciting fragments from the *A Concise Chinese-English Dictionary For Lovers* by Guo Xiaolu. The novel, which is set in London and describes the éducation sentimentale of a young Chinese woman from the country, is a ready reference for anyone who needs a hand in the languagelessness of love in East-West dialogue.

At her feet is a Maneki Neko or beckoning cat doll – a traditional Japanese symbol of good luck, which is now also popular in China. In this version, it is golden, a sign of wealth, and waves its left arm to attract many people. Facing it is another toy – a good old German dachshund – nodding and shaking its head, though it is impossible to tell whether it is agreeing or disagreeing or simply swaying in the wind. The two sit making eyes at one another, but their fur is too short for them to make a connection. And so they wave and wobble until – at the end of the performance – they are packed back into the dark props box before setting off on their return journey to Europe in a container.

Matthias Mersch
An excerpt from *Beijing Rundschau*,
the German-language edition of the
weekly news magazine *Beijing Review,* 21-11-2008
Translated by Vivien Smith

Facts about *china-hair-connection Beijing-Cologne*
Part 1, Cologne

Performers
Gerno Bogumil
Er Gao
Marianne Bettina Ernst
Deborah Gassmann
Snežana Golubović
Gong Zhonghui
Sun Yue Jie
Wang Zhiheng
Yang Yunzhi
Zhang Mengqi
Zhang Wei

Concept, direction, choreography, installations, overall management Angie Hiesl and Roland Kaiser
Costumes Rupert Franzen
Technical director Andy Semmler
Director's assistant and production assistant Aline Vásquez Keller
Assistant Anja Bosch
Special effects Andy Semmler, supported by Michael Reyl
Technical crew Gaby Boley, Eva Dönges, Timo Eckstein, Christoph Klöcker, Stefan Schmittblass, Ina Schulte-Krumpen
Technical construction David Braunisch, Co. f.punkt, Pit Paffen, Jan Frederic Schlamp

Project coordinator and organizer Astrid Lutz
Public and media relations Inga Dickel and freispiel Kulturagentur
Security Secura GmbH
Thirty helpers at the performance venue
Trainees Franziska Braunisch, Andrea Fricke, Lisa Hashemi
Simultaneous translation and Chinese translation / brochure Luo Ying
English translation / brochure Vivien Smith
Legal advice Reinhard Bergmann
Photo documentation Roland Kaiser
Graphic design Steffen Missmahl

Locations
Auditions tanzhaus nrw, Dusseldorf; Kunsthaus Rhenania
Rehearsals Kunsthaus Rhenania, Halle Kalk (Museum Ludwig), public and private spaces in the Eigelstein district, Kreuzkirche (former Protestant church)
Performance venue public and private spaces in the Eigelstein district

World premiere: 21 August 2008
22 August 2008, postponed due to weather to 24 August 2008 / 23 August 2008
Additional performances during the internationale tanzmesse nrw (dance fair) 28 August 2008 / 29 August 2008 / 30 August 2008
Performances started at 8 pm / Duration: 110 minutes

Text fragments *A Concise Chinese-English Dictionary For Lovers* by Guo Xiaolu, London: Vintage, 2008

Music *L'Internationale* by Jin Hao
CD Jin Hao – Opera Masks Drumming Out, Jinhao, 2007

Facts about *china-hair-connection Beijing-Cologne*
Part 2, Beijing

Performers
Gerno Bogumil
Er Gao
Deborah Gassmann
Snežana Golubović
Gong Zhonghui
Sun Yue Jie
Yang Yunzhi
Zhang Mengqi

Concept, direction, choreography, installations, overall management Angie Hiesl and Roland Kaiser
Costumes Rupert Franzen
Technical director Andy Semmler
Director's assistant and production assistant Aline Vásquez Keller
Production assistant Xu Yan
Production assistant and technical assistant Cheng Bo
Assistants He Yufan, Liu Chunyu, Pei Huifeng
Technical construction Bei An Mao Sheng Decorating
Simultaneous translation Cheng Bo, He Yufan, Pei Huifeng, Wawa, Xu Yan

Project coordinator and organizer Astrid Lutz
Coordinator Crossing Festival Pei Yanfeng
Technical director Crossing Festival Su Ming
Public and media relations Inga Dickel
Security The Red Yard watchmen
Eight helpers at the performance venue
English translation / brochure Vivien Smith
Chinese translation / brochure Luo Ying
Legal advice Reinhard Bergmann
Photo documentation Roland Kaiser
Graphic design Steffen Missmahl

Locations
Auditions Living Dance Studio / ccdworkstation, Caochangdi
Rehearsals and performance venue Red Yard, Caochangdi
Location manager of the Red Yard Mao Ran

Chinese premiere in Beijing
Participation at the Crossing Festival 10 October 2008
Additional performances 11 October 2008 / 12 October 2008
Performances started at 4 pm / Duration: 100 minutes

Text fragments *A Concise Chinese-English Dictionary For Lovers* by Guo Xiaolu, London: Vintage, 2008

Music *L'Internationale* by Jin Hao
CD Jin Hao – Opera Masks Drumming Out, Jinhao, 2007

Film documentation – Cologne and Beijing
Gerrit Busmanr, Angie Hiesl and Roland Kaiser
Director of photography in Cologne Gerrit Busmann
Directors of photography in Beijing Xie Lina, Luo Bing, Zou Xueping
Editing and postproduction Gerrit Busmann
Concept Angie Hiesl and Roland Kaiser
Premiere during the tanz nrw 09 festival in the Tanzmuseum Köln (Dance Museum Cologne) 17 May 2009

THANKS TO all those involved in the project in Beijing and Cologne for their dedication and commitment. We are particularly grateful to

Abasonic Group – imsu GmbH
Uta Atzpodien
Auto Bendheuer OHG
Beim Mäus, bar and restaurant, Eigelstein
Cologne City Council Culture Department
Deng Qiyue
Bernd Dudek and Ralf Feckler – Museum Ludwig, Cologne
Birgit Ellinghaus
Dieter Endemann – Protestant community in Cologne
Almuth Fricke
Marc Günther
Gerhardt Haag
Dr. Peter Hachenberg – Confucius Institute, Dusseldorf
Irmi Hiesl
Alfred Holtkott – HOTEL MADISON, Cologne
André Jolles
Paul Jürgens
Hedda Kage
Martin Kammann – Schauspiel Köln (Cologne Municipal Theatre)
The Kiosk at Eigelstein 29
Kölner Freiwilligen Agentur e.V. (volunteer agency)
Detlef Meyer, bike market and workshop
Bertram Müller – tanzhaus nrw, Dusseldorf
Claudius Nestvogel
Thomas Niepagenkemper
Qing Qing
Reiner Radke, Nikola Schetler, Otto Schneider – Gaffel Kölsch
Ren Lan
Dr. Nora Sausmikat
Michael Scholz
Karlheinz Schumacher and Patrick Turner – Cologne City Council Department of Bridge Engineering and Suburban Transport
Hans Sennekamp – pro fit
Dr. Ulrich S. Soénius
The Sundermann family
Thomas Thorausch
Anne and Wolfgang Tiedt
Zhong Chen

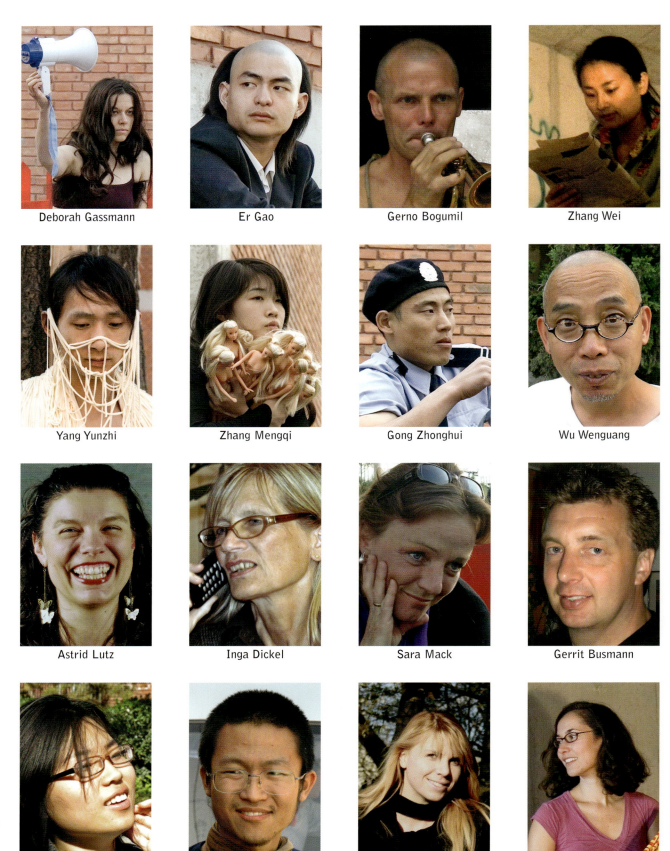

team

Wang Zhiheng   Marianne B. Ernst   Snežana Golubović   Sun Yue Jie

Wen Hui   Constance Vos   Dineke Koerts   Reinhard Bergmann

Pei Huifeng   Pei Yang Fang   He Yufan   Steffen Missmahl

Rupert Franzen   Andy Semmler   Roland Kaiser   Angie Hiesl

ARTISTIC TEAM

Angie Hiesl
Born in 1954, grew up in Venezuela, Perú and Germany, and has lived in Cologne since 1975. She is a director, choreographer, performance and installation artist and founder of the label **Angie Hiesl Produktion**.
Since the beginning of the 1980s she has presented her site-specific, interdisciplinary works, for which she has received numerous theatre and arts prizes. She is one of the first choreographers in Germany to exclusively develop site-specific choreographies.

Roland Kaiser
Born in 1958, has lived in Cologne since 1987.
He is a director, choreographer, performance and visual artist. Since 1993 he has realized numerous site-specific, interdisciplinary performance projects. Roland Kaiser also photographically documents all the projects developed by Angie Hiesl Produktion.

Angie Hiesl Produktion
Angie Hiesl and **Roland Kaiser** have enjoyed a longstanding artistic partnership. Since 1997 they have created and realized their interdisciplinary projects at non-artistic spaces in urban environments under the label Angie Hiesl Produktion. Hiesl and Kaiser's site-specific works temporarily transform public and private spaces into art spaces. Their artistic and performative interventions create new contexts and condense the special features of the locality, setting them in relation to social phenomena. The thematic coordinates are the relationship between the human body and space / architecture and people in their respective cultural, social, political, and global environment. The limitations and limitlessness of the human body are also central issues. In their concepts and highly original aesthetic forms of expression, Hiesl and Kaiser intriguingly re-arrange reality and provoke the senses, inviting the audience and passers-by alike to re-examine something they assumed to be familiar.
Hiesl and Kaiser communicate their art in workshops and lectures. Their works have been performed worldwide and have won multiple awards.
www.angiehiesl.de

Rupert Franzen – costume designer
Born in 1963. From 1985 to 1990 he studied art and design at the University of Applied Sciences in Cologne and attended classes in costume design led by Professor Elisabeth Vary. From 1993 to 1995 he was head of the costume department and also costume and stage designer at Dinslaken Regional Theatre. Since 1985 he has worked as a costume designer for fringe theatres, musicals and dance companies in Essen, Cologne, Bremen and Stuttgart and at various municipal playhouses and theatres in Germany (Schauspiel Köln, Oper Bonn, Stadttheater Bielefeld, Städtische Bühnen Osnabrück). He also shows his freelance work in the sphere of applied art and the visual arts in individual and group exhibitions. Costume designer for productions which won the 1998, 2004, 2006 NRW Festival Theaterzwang Prize and the 2002 Cologne Theatre Prize. He worked most recently for Angie Hiesl and Roland Kaiser in 2007 as a costume designer for *MACADAM* and in 2006 for *… and HAIR and HAIR and HAIR and …* .

PERFORMERS

Gerno Bogumil – performance artist, musician and sound artist
Born in Germany in 1961. Gerno Bogumil works as a performance artist and musician (trumpet, bass, percussion), appearing nationally and internationally. Since 1996 he has worked regularly with the music groups The Absurd, Intermission, Bogumil-Zierold-Duo and ADAM NOIDELT Missiles, amongst others. He has appeared as a soloist in project-related works, for example at KlangDrang Festival – Festival für unerhörte Musik (Festival of Unheard Music), the Altstadtherbst cultural festival in Dusseldorf and at exhibition openings. At the beginning of the 1980s, he was a performer and musician with the legendary performance group Minus Delta T. In 2003 he participated in *Windstoss*, an artistic quayside spectacle by and with Fantome-Pieds-Nus (Berlin). Since 1986 he has worked artistically with Angie Hiesl and since 1997 also with Angie Hiesl and Roland Kaiser in various projects, including *… and HAIR and HAIR and HAIR and …* in 2006 and *MACADAM* in 2007.

何其沃 **Er Gao (He Qiwo)** – dancer
Born in Guangdong, China in 1985. His real name is He Qiwo. He trained as a dancer at the Hong Kong Academy for Performing Arts (HKAPA), at the China Guang Dong Dance School (Modern Dance) and at the China Guang Dong Art School (Chinese Dance). Er Gao was awarded a Duchess of Kent International Scholarship and a scholarship from the Hong Kong Academy For Performing Arts. He has taken part as a dancer and performer in contemporary dance companies and rap formations in China and abroad. For several years now, Er Gao has also created his own dance pieces and works as a lecturer and teacher.
blog.sina.com.cn/eagleho9

Marianne Bettina Ernst – performer
Born in Germany in 1980. Master of Science, currently doctoral candidate in Molecular Medicine. Her passion is ballet and jazz dance. She is an internationaly renowned model with calf-long hair. She has worked with renowned artists, including Andrea Cochetti, Jasmin Taiebi, Bodo Jaster, Frank Müllert und Mátyás Varga.
www.amazing-hair.de

Deborah Gassmann – dancer
Born in Switzerland in 1982. She studied classical and modern dance at the Ecole de danse Duse in Lucerne before receiving further dance training at the Folkwang Academy in Essen. She has danced for Stefan Brinkmann, Rodolpho Leoni, Irina Loretz, Ben J. Riepe and Lior Shneior, amongst others.

Snežana Golubović – performance artist
Born in Belgrade, Serbia in the same year in which The Rolling Stones rocked the world with their hit *(I Can't Get No) Satisfaction*. She grew up with the Belgrade Alternative Scene (BAS), listened to Ekatarina Velika, read Danilo Kiš, visited BITEF (Belgrade International Theatre Festival) and the FEST film festival, studied drama, wrote about music and film and presented her own radio and television programs. In 1992 she moved to Germany, where she studied theatre, film and media in Frankfurt. From 2002 to 2004 she was personal assistant to Marina Abramović. She worked as an independent actor / performer with directors such as Alexander Brill, Dirk Hauser, Saskia Boddeke and Peter Greenaway. She put on her own performances at a number of venues, including the Van Gogh Museum Amsterdam in 2005, the Avignon Theatre Festival in 2005 and the 2007 Venice Biennale. She worked as a performer with Angie Hiesl and Roland Kaiser in *... and HAIR and HAIR and HAIR and ...*, 2006 and in *MACADAM*, 2007.

巩中辉 **Gong Zhonghui** – dancer
Born in China in 1981. From 1993 to 1999 he studied at the Jiangsu Province Culture and Art School in Wuxi. From 1999 to 2000 he worked as a dancer at the City Dance Troupe in Wuxi. From 2002 to 2006 he studied choreography at the Beijing Dance Academy. In January 2007 he performed in the Beijing Modern Dance Company and since June 2007 he has been working at the Paper Tiger Drama Studios, Beijing.

孙跃颉 **Sun Yue Jie** – dancer
Born in Yunnan province, China in 1975. Studied at the Beijing Dance Academy, Directing Department. After graduating, she worked as a lecturer for folk dance at the Guangdong Dance School. She is currently studying for a Master of Arts in Directing at the Beijing Dance Academy, where she has created many of her own works.

杨云志 **Yang Yunzhi** – dancer
Born in Hunan province, China in 1982. Trained as a dancer at Hunan Jishou University and the Guangdong Dance School, amongst others. Since 2005 he has worked as a freelance dancer and has been manager of the Beijing City Contemporary Dance Company since 2007. His first cooperation with Angie Hiesl Produktion was in 2006 during the Shanghai Fringe Festival in the work in progress performance project *...public hair...* .
blog.sina.com.cn/u/1266531600

章梦奇 **Zhang Mengqi** – dancer
Born in Hubei, China in 1987. She studied dance and dance education at the Central National University Beijing, graduating with distinction, and also studied modern dance in the Beijing Modern Dance Group. In 2002 her performances included dancing in the large-scale dance poem *Life Green*.
In March 2008 she performed in the Sino-Japanese exchange project *We're Gonna Go Dancing !!* with her piece *Plundering*.

张薇 **Zhang Wei** – performer
Born in Jiangsu, China in 1981. From 2000 to 2005 she took a Vocal Studies course at the Art Academy of Nanjing and graduated from there with a Bachelor of Music. She has been studying Musicology at the University of Cologne since 2005.

王志恒 **Wang Zhiheng** – performer
He was born in Dalian, China in 1980 and studied Marketing in China. In 2005 he came to Germany. Since 2006 he has been studying Business Administration at the University of Cologne.

TECHNICAL TEAM AND ORGANIZATION

Aline Vásquez Keller – director´s assistant
and production assistant
Born in Leipzig, Germany in 1981. Performance artist and community performance teacher. She obtained a BA degree in Performance and Stage Design from the University of Wales. She has been involved as a project manager, workshop trainer and assistant director in numerous national and international productions, among others, at the Theater im Bauturm, Cologne, the Theater 1000 Hertz and in *can do can dance*, Hamburg by Royston Maldoom.
www.alinekeller.theaterblogs.de

Andy Semmler – technical director and special effects
Stage design and technical direction, Landestheater Castrop-Rauxel, Forum Inter Art, Cocomico and since 1998 Stunksitzung (cabaret) in Cologne. Decorative sculpture: Expo 2000 – Deutsche Bahn, *Postbulle – Börsengang der Post*, 2005 *Football Globe II*, André Heller, rock landscape in the tiger enclosure at Wuppertal Zoo. Technical manager for tour performances by Dirk Bach (1992-1994), Cordula Stratmann (2001-2005), 3Gestirn (2001-2003), Wilfried Schmickler (since 2003) and Didi Jünemann (since 1994). Andy Semmler has worked as technical director for Angie Hiesl and Roland Kaiser since 2001.

程博 **Cheng Bo** – production assistant
and technical assistant in Beijing
Born in Tianjin, China in 1983. He studied at the State University of Film and Television in St. Petersburg, Russia. Today, he lives and works as a filmmaker and photographer in Beijing.

许岩 **Xu Yan** – production assistant in Beijing
Born in China. Xu Yan, called Alice, studied Language at the Beijing Language and Culture University. She obtained a BA in Chinese Literature in 2004 and received the Best Volunteers Zhenhai Award. In 2007 she was director´s assistant and interpreter for different stage plays. She also taught English and Chinese. In 2008 she took part in the Access Workshop for Teachers in the United States and was awarded a Teacher Training Certificate from Oregon State University. In 2009 she taught English at the Beijing Bainian Vocational School and was a visual arts teaching assistant at the Beijing City International School.

Astrid Lutz – project coordinator and organizer
Business graduate, event manager. In 2002 she assumed responsibility for project management and organization at Angie Hiesl Produktion. Since 2004 she has been in charge of a number of cultural projects on a freelance basis, including: organization of *dance meets differences* (a dance project in Kenya, Brazil and Germany) by DIN A13 tanzcompany (2004-2005), organization of *kulturdifferenztanz* and *crossing dance festival* by DIN A13 tanzcompany (2006), management and PR for the Taubenhaucher improvisational theatre (2005-2007) and organization of *GROMA*, urban sound installation by Michael Scholz (2007).
www.arts-org.de

Inga Dickel – public and media relations manager
for Cologne and Beijing
Since 2004 she has been responsible for national and international management and for public and media relations at Angie Hiesl Produktion.

Sara Mack – public and media relations manager
for Cologne
freispiel Kulturagentur is a culture management agency. Sarah Bergh and Sara Mack are mediators, idea creators and service providers for artistic, cultural and educational projects. They develop and realize projects commissioned by public authorities, private companies and artists from a wide range of disciplines.
www.freispiel.info

Gerrit Busmann – film documentation
He is a creator of TV and video productions in Cologne, Germany. As a TV journalist specializing in the arts, he has produced numerous features for the WDR network since 1986, most notably more than 350 editions of *Premierenreport*. He also works as a freelance director of photography, editor and producer of documentaries in the area of dance, theatre and performance art. He has collaborated with Angie Hiesl and Roland Kaiser since the late 1980s.

PROJECT PARTNERS

china-hair-connection Beijing-Cologne is a production by Hiesl+Kaiser GbR. Partners of the project are the Living Dance Studio, Borneoco and Angie Hiesl Produktion. Co-organizer of the performances in Beijing was the Goethe-Institut China.

Living Dance Studio, Beijing (China)
Living Dance Studio (LDS) is a cultural centre in Beijing's Chaoyang District. It comprises an international group of professional Chinese artists involved in dance, performance, theatre, literature, music and film. The LDS does not receive any state support. It is headed by the choreographer and dancer Wen Hui and the documentary filmmaker and director Wu Wenguang.
LDS's mission is to establish a freelance cultural scene and to bring the main features of contemporary dance, dance theatre and performance art in China into the public domain. Furthermore, LDS is creating an archive about dance, theatre and performance for the further training of students and other interested parties. LDS sees itself as a centre for exchanging ideas in order to reinforce the sense of cultural identity between Chinese and foreign artists.
Since 2005 Living Dance Studio has cooperated with Angie Hiesl Produktion in the form of workshops and lectures by Angie Hiesl and Roland Kaiser in Beijing. Since 2007 it has cooperated on *china-hair-connection Beijing-Cologne*.
www.ccdworkstation.com

Borneoco, Amsterdam (Netherlands)
Borneoco was established on 1 May 1997 by Constance Vos and Dineke Koerts. They are curators, organizers and producers of cultural events, festivals and exchange programs, focusing on contemporary performing arts, film and video from non-Western societies. In 2005 they established the CultureXpress Foundation in orcer to give their partners in China more direct support. Angie Hiesl and Roland Kaiser worked with Borneoco on different projects in China from 2005 to 2008.
www.borneoco.nl

Goethe-Institut China, Beijing
Co-organizer Beijing
www.goethe.de/china

Angie Hiesl Produktion, Cologne (Germany)
For details, see page 124
www.angiehiesl.de

AUTHORS

Dorothée Bauerle-Willert
Born in Göppingen, Germany in 1951. Read Art History, Philosophy and German studies at Tübingen and Marburg. Study visit to the Warburg Institute in London. 1980 dissertation *Ghost stories for the Fully Adult. Commentary on Aby Warburg's Bilderatlas Mnemosyne*. Assistant at the Staatliche Kunsthalle Baden-Baden. 1983 director of the Society for Contemporary Art in Bremen. 1983-1990 deputy director of Ulm Museum. 1990 lecturer in Art History at the Académia de Bellas Artes in Asunción de Paraguay and in German Literature at the Universidad Nacional. 1993-1996 teaching and curatorial work in Montevideo, Uruguay. 1996-2000 guest professor at the University of Art in Tallinn, Estonia. 2000-2007 professorships in Skopje, Macedonia and in Belgrade, Serbia. Since 2007 she has lived in Berlin and lectures at the University of Cologne.

Lothar Kittstein
Born in Trier, Germany in 1970. State examination in German Language and Literature Studies, History and Philosophy in 1997, conferral of a doctorate in 2001. 2002-2004 headhunter at a consultancy, Bonn. Since 2002 he has been a freelance author for stage plays and theatre texts and freelance dramatic advisor. *In a moonlit winter night* was presented during the Autorentheatertage in the Thalia Theater, Hamburg in 2005. Since 2005 he has written stage plays for theatres in Osnabrück, Marburg, Trier, Cologne, Bonn and Bochum. In 2005 he was awarded the Theatre Prize for Children by the Frankfurt Authors Foundation. In 2006 he won the Würth Prize for Literature. He has written contracting works for the municipal theatres in Bonn, Aachen and Frankfurt. He lives in Bonn.

Dineke Koerts and Constance Vos, Borneoco
For details, see above
www.borneoco.nl

Matthias Mersch
Born in Garmisch-Partenkirchen, Germany in 1960. MA in Social Anthropology, History of Religions and Japanology from Tübingen University in 1988. 1989-1990 ERASMUS Fellow in Rome, Italy. MA in History of Natural Sciences and Technology, History of Knowledge and Social and Economic History from Munich Technical University and Ludwig Maximilian University in 2009. Documentary filmmaking since 1988. From 1991 to 2004 he worked for the Bavarian Broadcasting (BR). Since 2007 he has been an editor of the *Beijing Rundschau*, the German-language edition of the weekly news magazine *Beijing Review* in Beijing.

在此特别鸣谢　A special thank you goes to
吴文光　　　Wu Wenguang
文慧　　　　Wen Hui
毛然　　　　Mao Ran
　　　　　　Dineke Koerts
　　　　　　Constance Vos

Publisher: Reinhard Bergmann

Produced by Hiesl+Kaiser GbR in cooperation
with Angie Hiesl Produktion and Emons, Cologne
www.angiehiesl.de
www.emons-verlag.de

PICTURE CREDITS
All photos of *china-hair-connection Beijing-Cologne* by Roland Kaiser
Exception: page 109 small photo below right by Angie Hiesl

Additional photos:
Other projects in the *HAIR cycle*: Photos by Roland Kaiser
Pages 1, 3, 4, 18, 23, 25 *Standpoint Beijing*, Beijing 2008
Pages 7 (above), 8, 9, 12 *... and HAIR and HAIR and HAIR and ...*,
Cologne 2006, a collaboration between Schauspiel Köln and Angie Hiesl
Produktion (Performers: Snežana Golubović, Julia Riera, Ella L'Étang)
Pages 7 (below) 13, 17 *...public hair...*, Shanghai 2006,
work in progress project (Performers: Yin Yun Lin, Yang Yunzhi)

The *HAIR cycle* was created by Angie Hiesl and Roland Kaiser

Further photos:
Pages 118, 119: Roland Kaiser
Exception: page 118 – left to right: No. 9 Stefan Klein, No. 10 Paul Jürgens,
No. 11 Marc Hanzer, No. 12 Gerrit Busmann, No. 15 Lukas Wolff
Page 119 – left to right: Nos. 6,7 private, No. 9 Andy Semmler, No. 12 private,
No. 15 Angie Hiesl

Editors in chief, concept: Angie Hiesl, Roland Kaiser
Editorial work: Inga Dickel
Organization: Astrid Lutz
Graphic design: Steffen Missmahl AGD

Authors: Dr. Dorothée Bauerle-Willert, Dr. Lothar Kittstein, Dineke Koerts
and Constance Vos / Borneoco, Matthias Mersch
Translators: Vanessa Anderson, Vivien Smith, Urle U, Dr. Richard Volk,
Luo Ying, Wang Zhiheng
Proofreader: Elisabeth Sparla
Printed in Germany, February 2010 by Grafisches Centrum Cuno, Calbe
Printed on 170 g/qm Luxo Art Silk
Print run 1,750 copies, of which 1,200 with DVD film documentation
© Hermann-Josef Emons Verlag
　Alle Rechte vorbehalten
© Texts by the authors
© Photos by the photographers
© 2010 VG Bild-Kunst, Bonn, for the works of Angie Hiesl and Roland Kaiser

No part of this book may be reproduced in any form or by any means,
electronic or mechanical, including photocopying, without permission in writing
from the publisher.

ISBN 978-3-89705-736-4

We would like to thank all our funders and sponsors
without whose support *china-hair-connection
Beijing-Cologne* could not have been accomplished.

Project and documentation funded by

Project kindly supported by

HOTEL MADISON, Köln

Amt für Brücken- und
Stadtbahnbau Köln

Media partner